Crisis Management - Principles, Roles and Application

Edited by Carine Yi

Published in London, United Kingdom

Crisis Management - Principles, Roles and Application
http://dx.doi.org/10.5772/intechopen.100653
Edited by Carine Yi

Contributors
Serge Banyongen, Marcus T. Anthony, Gabriel Lele, Rita W. Shilisia, Hillary Bett, Job Lagat, Xiao Wang, Qiudi Wu, Yi-Hui Christine Huang, James P. Welch

First published in London, United Kingdom, 2023 by IntechOpen
IntechOpen is the global imprint of INTECHOPEN LIMITED, registered in England and Wales, registration number: 11086078, 5 Princes Gate Court, London, SW7 2QJ, United Kingdom

British Library Cataloguing-in-Publication Data
A catalogue record for this book is available from the British Library

Additional hard and PDF copies can be obtained from orders@intechopen.com

Crisis Management - Principles, Roles and Application
Edited by Carine Yi
p. cm.
Print ISBN 978-1-80356-491-3
Online ISBN 978-1-80356-492-0
eBook (PDF) ISBN 978-1-80356-493-7

Meet the editor

Dr. Carine J. Yi is a Senior Research Fellow and geographic information systems (GIS) analyst at R. Park & Associates Inc. She obtained a master's degree in Environmental Science (Urban Planning, 1996) and a Ph.D. in Hazard Engineering from the University of Tsukuba, Japan, in 2013. She obtained her GIS Application Specialist Diploma (Graduate Program) from Sir Sandford Fleming College, Ontario, Canada, in 2009. Dr. Yi joined the Institute of International Disasters (IRIDES) at Tohoku University as an assistant professor after she worked at the National Institute of Environmental Research (NIES) in Japan. Since then, she has researched a variety of topics, including the environmental impacts of climate change, large-scale disaster risks such as floods, landslides, sea-level rise and land degradation, and human-social impacts.

Contents

Preface

This volume is a collection of reviewed research chapters concerning developments in the field of crisis management. It includes scholarly contributions by experts organized into six chapters.

Chapter 1: "In the Eye of the Storm: Social Media and Crisis Management"

Chapter 2: "Revisiting Crisis Governance: Toward Collaborative Crisis Management"

Chapter 3: "Impact of Non-structural Flood Control Measures on Household Welfare in Bunyala Sub-County, Kenya"

Chapter 4: "Perspective Chapter: A Critical Futures Studies Perspective on Embodiment and the Crisis in Sensemaking"

Chapter 5: "Risk Perceptions Following a Substandard Vaccine Crisis in China: An Exploratory Approach to Substantiating the Tripartite Model"

Chapter 6: "The Challenges of Public Service Organizations in Emergency, Crisis, and Disaster Management"

This book is designed for scholars and specialists in the field of crisis management.

Carine Yi
R. Park & Associates Inc.,
Brampton, Canada

Chapter 1

In the Eye of the Storm: Social Media and Crisis Management

Serge Banyongen

Abstract

Social media, also called Web 2.0, is a generic term used to talk about applications that allow users to create, manipulate, and disseminate content as much as possible in real time. These applications allow for several possibilities that range from involvement to participation, communication, and collaboration of users. They allow everyone with minimal access to the Internet to publish, share, review, comment, and post items, such as mentions, comments, information, videos, and photos. In a crisis, social media becomes a double-edged sword. It can play an essential role during the prodromal, acute, chronic, and resolution phases of natural disasters and human-made crises. Social media can also be at the origin of the crisis or the reason for its amplification. Social media facilitates an increase of interactions between main actors at the center of a crisis. This chapter combines social media content analysis (opinion detection and sentiment analysis) with network analysis (ego network analysis) and nodes centrality assessment to critically evaluate how social media affects the crisis management process.

Keywords: social media, crisis informatics, ego network analysis, nodes centrality, content analysis

1. Introduction

The Internet has taken only a quarter of the time it took television channels to become popular. Users themselves set the trends and shape the framework in which organizations interact with them. Networks are driving the evolution of ever shorter messages, delivered with increasing frequency through a plurality of means and channels. Social media, also called Web 2.0, is a generic term used to refer to applications that allow their users to create, manipulate, and distribute content as much as possible in real time. These applications allow for several possibilities that range from involvement to participation, communication, and collaboration of users. They allow everyone with minimal access to the Internet to publish, share, review, comment, and post items, such as mentions, comments, information, videos, and photos. In this way, social media has distinguished itself from traditional websites. Kaplan et al. [1] have defined social media as "a group of internet-based applications that build on the ideological and technological foundations of Web 2.0 and allow the creation and exchange of user-generated content."

Indeed, with social media, the user can generate their own content, unlike with websites where they can only view it [2]. Social media companies have unleashed persuasive platforms that generate useful data for public debates, socialization, and information

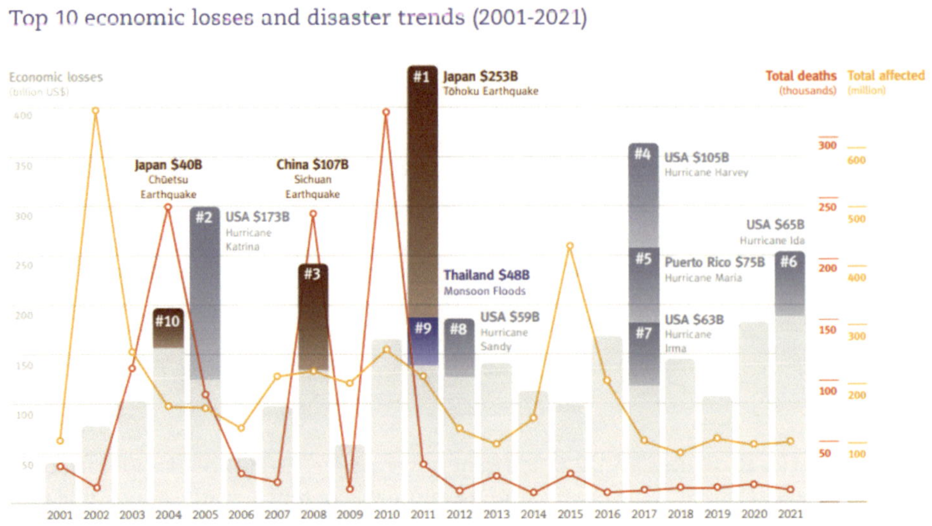

Figure 1.
This figure demonstrates the top 10 economic losses and disaster trends (source: 2021 disasters in numbers).

exchange, increasing their impact on daily lives [3]. Therefore, social media has substantially increased communication channels by allowing a constant interaction of information and opinions on a one-to-one, one-to-many, and many-to-many communicative basis [1, 4]. Social media has made it possible to blur boundaries and time by articulating ubiquity and multisharing. A story can spread virally to millions of people in just a few minutes [4]. Social media is characterized by interactivity, user-generated content, and multidirectional communication flows. With social media, the immediacy of information takes a new form as it arrives in real time. The public is no longer made of the distant spectators they once were. They do their own research on the authenticity of the news and sometimes influence the course of an event. In this sense, social media blurred the lines between the public and the audience. While for a long time, traditional media users acted as an audience (i.e., a passive spectator of the content diffused from these media), social media users now act as a public (i.e., they can influence the course of events through their interactions and have agency over events). Almost 5 billion people are connected to the Internet, and more than half of humanity (4.2 billion people) was connected to social media in 2021. The number of social media users grows by almost 13% yearly [5]. The progress of social media is the result of globalization. Ulrich Beck, a German sociologist, links globalization and crisis. In his famous theory on risk society, Beck argued that risk is inherent to modern society. This concept highlights social media's role as a bridge between globalization and crises. Social media has influenced crisis management in the health, corporate, nonprofit, religious, political, and natural disaster sectors [6].

As far as crises are concerned, just in 2021, a total of 432 catastrophic events were recorded (**Figure 1**). Floods dominated these events, with 223 occurrences, up from an average of 163 annual floods recorded across the 2001–2020 period. Storms were the second most frequently recorded disaster, with 121 events recorded in 2021[1].

These numbers do not account for technical and human-made crises; if we were to add them, the tally will be higher. In fact, the more people use social media, the more researchers and practitioners need to understand social media's impacts during

[1] Source: https://reliefweb.int/sites/reliefweb.int/files/resources/2021_EMDAT_report.pdf.

a crisis [7]. This chapter focuses on the links between social media and crises, through the following research question: How is social media used in crisis management? Before responding to this question, the chapter will first outline the applied methodological approach, then explain critical features of social media that are involved in crisis management, and finally describe the two primary analysis trends of crises on social media that are regularly presented in the literature: the content analysis and the network analysis.

2. Use of social media in crisis management

When a crisis strikes, the team in charge of responding is always in need of tools to manage the overflow of information by summarizing it. Time being of the essence, it is critical to collect, review and classify high-value messages while using them to identify and manage issues as they arise or are amplified [8]. Social media has developed features that allow the crisis management team to perform disaster forensics [9].

Social media is essential throughout the crisis management process, from early detection to recovery. Social media has increased the volume of connections and the proactive nature of exchanges, which actively participate in a new form of crisis management [10]. This is mainly due to the trust relationship that social media has created with traditional media [11]. Thus, according to Timothy Coombs [12], researchers in crisis communication spotted the potential of social media long before traditional communications research [13]. Social media allows for an increase in the interactions of key actors at the center of a crisis, such as citizens, local communities, and officials from different levels of government [14]. This configuration is found in a crisis because people often are confined to hiding places, constrained by, among other things, the triggering of barricaded confinement. Many used social media to communicate with their relatives and reassure them of their conditions. However, what interests us here is the social media activity that manages this crisis. Thus, as Rainer et al. [15] have demonstrated, social media can be used to allow for effective crisis management in several aspects. First, the management of risk and the prediction of its occurrence. Indeed, monitoring social media in real time increases the speed and efficiency with which emergency managers can react. Qualitative and quantitative processing of social media content increases the likelihood of predicting mass behavior and better understanding potential risks [16].

Social media also allows for better risk analysis. The information gathered helps first responders assess the danger of the situation, from the sharing of information and knowledge about the site on social media to the extent of the damage and the number of victims. This allows response teams to adequately plan for specific resources and determine the appropriate scope of work before starting tasks that need to be done, even before these teams arrive on the scene.

Once a crisis begins, social media can be used to coordinate the efforts of different working groups. The crisis management team members can be tasked according to their skills and the needs in the field. Social media has become an essential tool in the organization of post-crisis aid and allows the coordination of different community organizations that want to help with relief efforts. By providing adequate and real-time information to people affected by the crisis, social media enable people to understand the full scope of the crisis and signal the presence of crisis managers.

The rapid and real-time dissemination of information is undoubtedly one of the most used functions of social media in times of crisis. It can help save lives. In addition, it offers the advantage of reaching people who are cut off from traditional means of communication, especially in developing countries, where there are often more mobile phones than landlines and more smartphones and handhelds than desktop computers.

Social media also puts the role of first witnesses back at the center of the intervention. These act as citizen journalists and transmit valuable information with regular updates on the situation on the ground. Responders cannot be everywhere and often have limited resources [17].

Web 2.0 reorients the narrative about the crisis and the public at the heart of it, defining the causes, identifying the issues, and predicting the consequential impact [18]. Austin et al. [19] reflected on an organization's interactions over social media with its various audiences that produce, consume, and disseminate information during a crisis. Their model, called crisis communication through social media, has identified three types of social media to consider before, during, and after a crisis. Some influential creators create content and convey information about the situation that others consume. Followers consume the information provided by the creators. Inactive participants eventually use the data from the creators through word-of-mouth or through traditional media, which also follows creators. Researchers have recognized Twitter as playing a significant role during natural disasters.

Social media like Twitter provides a platform for the efficient organization of relief efforts and for strategic planning to avoid further human and material damage [20–22]. Web 2.0 technologies, social media, and media data mining are new technological forms that provide and gather information about the population affected by a crisis in an efficient manner [23, 24]. Social media help increase the flow of information between people directly affected and those close to them (family and friends). Most platforms have features that allow a user to let their loved ones know they are safe when a disaster occurs. This online reporting reassures others and better channels the search and rescue of those who need it most. Social media in crisis contexts allow for rapid updates on developments and continuous interaction with the community and neighborhood [25, 26].

In a crisis involving a sniper on the loose, it is wiser to use a phone to connect to social media than to speak in person, which would risk alerting the sniper of someone's presence and attempting to call for safety. This was the situation in the shootings of May 14, 2022, in Buffalo, New York, and, in the terrorist attack of September 21, 2013, at the Westgate shopping mall in Nairobi, Kenya. In these situations, it appears as if texting and updating the status through social media provided information to relatives while it is safer to do so than calling and using the voice, which could result in letting the sniper where you are hiding. In the case of the attack of January 9, 2015, against the kosher grocery store in the suburbs of Paris, France, social media have helped in crowdsourcing with people on the ground and played a key role in supplementing the 24 h/7 television cycle to contribute to the increase of the post-stress resulting from the trauma of being exposed physically to those events [27, 28].

Now that types of social media and users and their practicality during a crisis have been identified, and the next section will examine how social media can be used during a crisis. The answer to this *how* follows the phases that evolve chronologically during a crisis.

3. Methodology framework

This research uses the convergent parallel design method to triangulate multiple data sources using quantitative and qualitative approaches (QUAN +QUAL). From this, links between two phenomena such as crises and social media can be analyzed, and further interpret the combined results [29]. This approach comes from one of the most regularly used studies concerning social media [30]. This chapter conducts a systematic review of literature about crises and social media to determine the trends. A literature review, which examines existing research and information on a chosen field of study, is a crucial component of a research study. Fink's [31] definition of a research literature review as "a systematic, explicit, and reproducible method for identifying, evaluating, and synthesizing the existing body of completed and recorded work produced by researchers, scholars, and practitioners" corresponds to what we understand as a systematic literature review (p. 3). A systematic review is also a type of literature review. The main difference between a literature review and a systematic review is their focus on the research question; a systematic review is focused on a specific research question, whereas a literature review is not. The main objective of this type of research is to identify, review, and summarize the best available research on a specific research question. Systematic reviews are primarily used because reviewing existing studies is often more practical than conducting new research [32]. As adopted in this chapter, the review is predominantly descriptive to synthesize the critical aspects of using social media in crisis management.

The methodology followed was inspired by the work of Snelson [30], notably the four-stage approach, as well as the work of Kankanamge et al. [33], to highlight a comprehensive understanding of the use of social media in crisis (natural and man-made) management. The scientific articles used as a corpus in this chapter were selected from databases using four stages: pre-search, data collection, data cleaning, and analysis.

3.1 Data identification and collection

The research for this chapter was conducted from April to May 2022. Using Boolean search with keywords, such as social media and crisis management, articles were selected from the following databases: Academic Search Premier (n = 458); Applied Social Sciences Index and Statistics (n = 989); ProQuest (n = 370); Science Direct (n = 451); and Scopus (n = 693). These databases were chosen for their broad reach across multidisciplinary and interdisciplinary peer-reviewed journals. They also represent key research fields currently popular in scholarly publications. In studying links between social media and crisis, it is critical to research both the text and the context [34].

New specific keywords were included, such as social media and natural disasters, social media and organizational crisis, social media and reputation management, social media and image repair, crisis informatics, social media crisis communication, social media, and financial crisis, social media and political crisis, social media and economic crisis, social media and social crisis, and social media and scandal to reduce the scope of the research. The search was also restricted to the classic stages of crisis management as identified by Bundy et al. [35] and Lai & Wong, [36]: pre-crisis, crisis, and post-crisis. The articles retained for analysis were the ones with Boolean phrases, such as social media and crisis mitigation, social media and crisis preparedness, social media and crisis response, and social media and crisis recovery (**Table 1**). This research was also conducted to understand the influence of social media on the five "critical tasks" for leaders during crises, as identified by Boin et al. [37], namely: sense-making, decision-making, meaning-making, terminating, and learning.

Crisis management phases	Number of articles
Mitigation	11% (n = 24)
Preparedness	23% (n = 50)
Response	57% (n = 125)
Recovery	9% (n = 20)

Table 1.
Breakdown of the corpus based on crisis management phases.

3.2 Data cleaning

After filtering social media streams and reducing irrelevant information, the reference was identified by checking the title, abstract, key findings, and conclusion to ensure that each selected article was related to the research question. This methodological discrimination process brought down the total tally of articles from all databases to 219. Here is the following classification of articles based on the crisis management process:

3.3 Results

Content analysis was used to assess the corpus. "Content analysis is a research technique that is based on measuring the amount of something (violence, negative portrayals of someone, etc.) in a representative sampling of some mass-mediated popular form of art" ([38], p. 25). The "content" refers to words, meanings, pictures, symbols, ideas, themes, or any message that can be communicated. In content analysis, a systematic sample of texts is used in the study, and classification systems are devised to identify different features of the text, which are then counted with an emphasis on objectivity and reliability. This is done to describe the substance characteristics of message content, to describe the form characteristics of message content, to make inferences about audiences of content, and to predict the effects of content on audiences [39].

In the case of this research, content analysis was mainly used to find meaningful links between social media and the crisis management process, which prompted an assessment of the reliability of those two factors in the corpus using the kappa Cohen coefficient [40]. Cohen's kappa coefficient is a statistical measurement that calculates the level of agreement between two variables according to a formula. As a general rule, kappa is always less than or equal to 1 [41]. When kappa is less than or equal to 0.20, the level of agreement between the variables is poor. This agreement is fair when the kappa is between 0.20 and 0.40; it is moderate if kappa is between 0.40 and 0.60; it is good when the kappa is between 0.60 and 0.80, and it is very good if the coefficient is between 0.80 and 1. The coding of the corpus was conducted using NVivo and R software until an 0.80 coefficient was obtained. Case studies are by far the most used approach in the corpus, with 64% (n = 140), while for data collection techniques, the content analysis, including literature reviews, accounts for 47% (n = 103). Next comes focus groups (28% n = 61), interviews (12% n = 26), surveys (8% n = 17), and finally fieldwork and observations (5% n = 11).

The corpus studied shows Twitter as the most used platform representing 43%, highlighting its real-time capacities to provide useful data as the crisis outspread, thus improving situation awareness [42]. Some applications, such as WhatsApp, are also widely used and are part of the 15% of the corpus represented under the terms specialized platforms. In most cases, the literature revealed the use of combined platforms, such as Twitter and Facebook, Facebook and Instagram, or links from the three abovementioned platforms to YouTube. It is worth mentioning that the total of platforms used surpassed 100% because some studies in the selected corpus combined platforms for their research.

As per the platforms, the results were observed as shown in **Figure 2**.

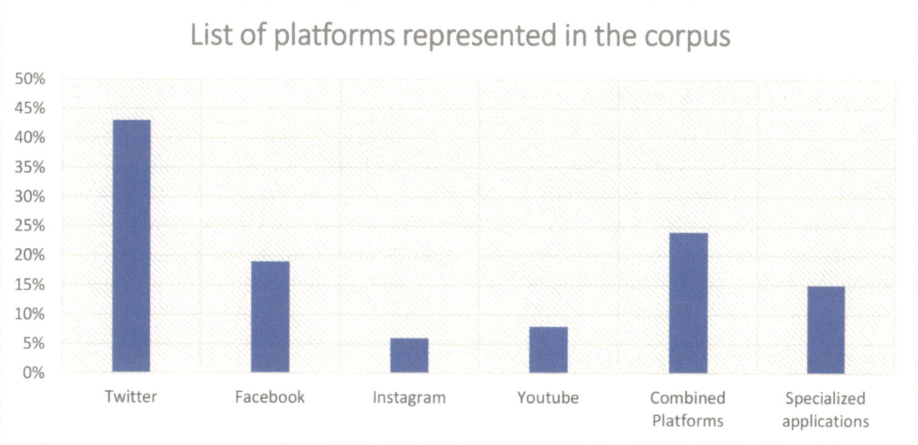

Figure 2.
List of social media platforms represented in the corpus.

Based on these findings, the literature provides tools and processes to assess data during the crisis on Facebook and Twitter, the most used platforms.

3.3.1 Data analysis through twitter

Twitter is a tool that has not always been used to its full potential during crises. Indeed, if citizens are massively present, their number increases substantially during a crisis, and some governments have often been reluctant to use this tool [43]. In addition to all the data identified above for Facebook and Twitter, during a crisis, it is the place from which rumors start that can impact the organization's ability to resolve the crisis and, later, its reputation. This is why the analysis of network interaction seems the most interesting. To determine this, several researchers use NodeXL, a network in the form of a list point to symbolize the relationship that exists not only between Twitter users but especially their interaction on a particular piece of content [44–46]. Each action performed on Twitter leaves traces that form a network. NodleXL makes it possible to highlight the connection networks of Twitter users. This tool uses the Clauset-Newman-Moore algorithm to divide network users into subgroups and generate graphs that identify connections between users [45].

Twitter's communication interface is quite flexible and allows for the exchange and communication through words with a more significant number of users, even if they do not follow each other. They are following each other and are not in the same network. Accounts on Twitter are both public, that is, visible to all, including those who are not registered as members, or else private, that is, visible only to those in one's network [47, 48]. During a crisis, information is gathered by tracking keywords and tweets made from those words. This was seen during the Boston terrorist attack with the keyword #Bostonstrong, among others.

Twitter allows access to public tweets through two practical tools: the application programming interface (API) and streaming, enabling one to see the tweets at any time and see them as they are written. There can be three types of analysis: activity analysis, network analysis, and content analysis [47].

The calculation of statistics and indicators describing the activities Twitter activity captured in a dataset at a particular time relies primarily on processing these datasets based on specific communication profiles. The additional filtering of the data during a certain time, user, or keyword evaluation may also be necessary to better understand the activity on Twitter better.

The analysis of Twitter activity can be done temporarily. It then includes the overall volume of tweets plus the hourly volume of different types of tweets over time (original tweets, replies, unpublished retweets, revised retweets, tweets containing URLs, etc.). This analysis is also based on the volume of specific keywords (or clusters of keywords over time), the number of active users over some time (day, hour, day of the week) period (day, hour, minute), and the average number of tweets per user over a while.

3.3.2 Data analysis through Facebook

There are four primary actions on Facebook. You can either post a piece of information or a video, like someone's post, comment on it or share it with your network of friends and admirers. The ability to spread is one of the things to measure with Facebook accounts. Outreach is an aggregation of the total number of pages, likes, friends, and people talking about it, those who spread the information back in turn, and the click-through rate obtained [49]. From a post, one can evaluate the viral nature of the data by determining the number of people who have shared it. This allows us to know the type of post that pushes the audience to action, however small it may be. Obtaining such data is crucial in post-crisis analysis because it gives an idea of the quality of information to look for in times of crisis [50, 51]. Applications such as Facebook Insights also provide information about page views by unique visitors, that is, those who came directly to the Facebook page without being driven there by an ad.

The engagement rate is generally one of the most calculated data on Facebook. It measures how well an organization interacts with its audience on Facebook. It is data that is calculated post-ante. It is an equation that divides the number of people who clicked, liked, commented, or shared the post by the number of people who have seen it. This aspect is critical during a crisis when you want to calculate the relevance of the diffusion of information [52]. It is necessary to transcend the reach rate (the number of people who have seen the post) because many accounts are fake or robotic and automatically generate traffic without the expected impact. The rate is a useful measure to evaluate the quality of the information content generated on Facebook. Only the account administrator can obtain it.

4. Key features of social media in crisis management

Several essential aspects of social media need to be assessed to understand its role in managing crises properly. One of these crucial aspects is the concept of a network, which, when studied, helps indicate how information is created.

4.1 Networks

Throughout history, networks have always been part of society, existing at the center of power [53]. They suggest how people have lived in society through their form and how people are connected through various positions. Indeed, people seem tailored to influence and interact with one another, and our brains seem wired to seek connectivity with others [54]. Linking globalization and the evolution of the information and communication technology of (ICT), Manuel Castells [55] explained that new relations using ICT have emerged, creating a new social structure. The analysis of social ties is a field that has grown in importance while establishing the sociology of information and communication techniques [56]. A social network is a social structure composed of individuals (or organizations) called "nodes," linked by one or more specific types of interdependence, such as friendship; kinship; common interest; financial exchange; aversion; sexuality; or relationships of belief, knowledge, or prestige [57]. Scholarly literature has shown that it is impossible to manage a crisis through social media without a social network analysis (SNA), which refers to the regularities in the patterning of relationships among individuals, groups, or organizations. When a crisis arises, it is critical to understand how information circulates within a network, wherever the information has started or if social media simply amplify it.

4.2 Homophily

Although definitions of homophily differ in their specificity, their basic theoretical intent agrees that it is "the degree to which interacting pairs of individuals are similar in certain attributes" ([58], p. 402). Homophily is also "the tendency of individuals to interact with similar individuals" ([59], p. 463). Fincham explained that homophily acquires meaning for the individuals involved and thus influences their social interaction (2019). One of the important observations made by social scientists is this tendency in social groups to connect similar people (after all, birds of a feather flock together). This tendency significantly affects the values derived from social media, where people often encounter similar voices and interact with like-minded people. Homophily has predictive power in social media, so researchers can predict real-life friendships by looking at online interactions, common interests, and location [60]. This concept can be seen as correlated with the question: Who social media users view to be trustworthy in a crisis? It explains how information circulates during a crisis and key phenomena such as fake news and echo chambers.

4.3 Bubble filters

Bubble filter is the concept by which algorithms track your activities online and systematically arrange the content you have access to base on your preferences. These filters structure people's online experience, isolating them from the information they have not previously expressed interest in [61]. The bubble filters are based on the selective exposure theory [62]. When managing a crisis, bubble filters represent a serious threat in the CMT attempt to reach out to targeted audiences through social media as the filters might not allow the information to go through their bubble of preferences [63]. While networks, homophily, and bubble filters are hindering the reach, echo chambers' next concept impacts the message's persuasiveness during a crisis.

4.4 Echo chambers

Integral to the echo chamber is the idea that opinions in the network are polarized with self-reinforcing nodes [64]. Online users decide to isolate themselves in the worlds of a shared imagination [65]. Recent studies have shown that online users tend to select the information that adheres to their belief systems, ignore information that does not, and join groups—that is, echo chambers—centered around a shared narrative. This concept can explain how it was difficult during the COVID-19 pandemic to present rational arguments against conspiracy theories [66–69]. Information circulation is not the only critical aspect of social media related to a crisis; the speed of information travel is also essential. Other key features that link social media to a crisis include virality and buzz.

4.5 Virality

The concept of virality is borrowed from medicine and related to the proliferation of harmful viruses inside the human body, or in this case, society. Metcalfe's law [70], which famously characterizes many of the effects seen in communication technologies and networks, from the Internet and social networking to the World Wide Web, could explain virality as a dynamic of information transmission speed on social media. The law states that the value of a telecommunications network is proportional to the square of the number of connected users of the system. According to Huberman et al. [71], virality is related to mimetics since it boils down to sharing and looking for information that other people are already looking for and sharing. People online are hungry for novelty and anything that sounds new.

4.6 Buzz

Crises on social media are by-products of bad buzz. This is another expression to designate electronic word-of-mouth that has the power to hinder an organization's reputation. Since communication on social media happens in real time, most users have the privilege of being news breakers organizations managing crises should pay careful attention to that phenomenon.

Now that features of social media with the power to impact crises have been outlined, it is time to look at how social media, according to the literature, manage crises.

5. Crisis watch: social media monitoring

There are several factors to consider when monitoring the possibility of a crisis on social media. It involves tracking specific elements on the social media horizon to identify those that could be problematic. This monitoring provides crucial information in real time and on a continuous basis, covering controversial topics. At the same time, it gives access to new or hidden elements that emerge in conversations that an organization previously ignored, giving a whole new perspective on the subject.

Social media monitoring is an integral element of risk communication and, therefore, an essential component of any crisis communication strategy. Web 2.0 is where reputational risks are high, so it is advisable for 24/7 monitoring [72]. The purpose of monitoring is to identify radical opinions and elements that could damage an organization's reputation and thus trigger a crisis [73] and identify all negative opinions in a general way [74]. In this way, social media monitoring can track the trajectory of comments and discussion patterns that emerge from different topics accompanying main comments, especially the profiles of the most influential people. Such a predisposition already draws the cartography of the action in a crisis. Time is the scarcest commodity during a crisis. The continuous monitoring of the networks allows one to know how to orient oneself during a crisis.

The social media monitoring process needs to be segmented into several steps to be effective [47, 75, 76]. First, the preparation is done based on objectives established beforehand in close connection with the organization's mission. The proposal is not to monitor citizens' private conversations but rather the information they have chosen to make public on social media. Although the first type of surveillance is espionage, the second type belongs to the field of strategic communication.

Preparing for a crisis takes an organization through the process of defining a crisis. Potential risks are identified for each organization in the crisis communication plan. The preparation phase also requires assessing the resources necessary to ensure adequate monitoring. Once preparation is done, the monitoring itself begins. At this stage, the main focus is on collecting critical data. As with any information-gathering exercise, it is essential to use an appropriate method. This can be done manually using Boolean operators or search engines [77]. The next step is to analyze the information. This can be done in a statistical, metric, or specific way on the activities, content, or network. This process is operationalized from the applications of the program interface designated API, which is a system of tools and resources in an operating system that allows an operating system to enable developers to create software applications such as Tweet Archivist, Tweetdeck, the Hootsuite galaxy of Hootsuite, Netvibes, and Trackur APIs [76]. Facebook and Twitter both offer APIs for data search, as do some free search engines such as Social Mention. Monitoring is an essential tool in the decision-making process in times of crisis [78–80]. In crisis cases, such as mass shootings, perpetrators have been vocal on social media for some time and could have been spotted with proper monitoring [81].

To summarize, following [76], a textual analysis that allows for understanding user opinions is necessary for monitoring. This requires specialists who work 24/7 by combining a manual approach with the appropriate software. Monitoring social media with essential information monitoring tools is critical in crisis management.

6. Response and recovery phases: social media analysis

The following section adopts a normative approach because, in the literature, the authors advised the crisis management team (CMT) on harvesting social media's power to mitigate the crisis effects.

Social media increases information and knowledge during a crisis, whether the public is affected or not [82]. After social media monitoring comes social media analysis, which is the development and evaluation of tools to visualize, collect, and track social media data based on the particular requirements of a target application [83]. There are different types of data: The so-called structured data include the sociodemographic elements of the user; thematic data include content such as likes, comments, shares, and more; unstructured data can be stored and include, among other things, the identity of the ad, timestamp, username (of the author), the content of the posting, sometimes content, and occasionally even the type of posting. It is, therefore, advisable to adopt some practical approaches to social media analysis, such as thematic or trend-based analysis, opinion, and sentiment analysis, the structural method [84], or the ecosystem approach [85]. When responding to a crisis, collecting meaningful information and tracking its propagation are critical for a crisis management team [86].

Social media analysis during a crisis shows a clear difference in focus in the literature based on the research approaches where social science authors produce more qualitative research focusing on content analysis: opinion detection and sentiment analysis. In contrast, authors from the computers and health sciences fields emphasize quantitative research using structural methods with network analysis and computational methods as critical aspects of understanding how social media could be used to assess the crisis dynamic.

One of the key limitations in the literature is that there is little to no exchange and discussion between researchers and, more important, no comprehensive approach to analyses of response and recovery through social media. The following section will be divided into two main parts: It will first present the quantitative and then qualitative methods as they appear in the literature review.

6.1 Qualitative data analyses (QDA)

This section is about the research that displayed analysis of the impacts of social media on crises that mostly focus on text-based data. They describe the use of words, assess non-numeric data information, and explain the nature and deployment of key concepts and ideas related to the topic.

6.1.1 Content analysis

Opinion detection: During a crisis, social media can be used to gather necessary information, especially with the detection of opinions. The crisis management team struggled to convince people to abandon their homes in natural disasters such as the California wildfires in the United States. An opinion survey can help identify the fears and needs of people caught in the middle of a crisis like this one. Opinion research uses a thematic approach and requires an analysis process of social media content.

For this purpose, there are two main approaches [72]:

1. Natural language processing analyzes representations and implicit meanings based on a vector of texts and meanings, leading to identifying degrees of positive or negative opinions of texts produced in social media.

2. The semantic web approach detects explicit representations of the domain based on the semantic annotations that trace the ontology of the text from keywords or tags.

Both approaches focus on detecting opinions on social media to provide senior executives with a rational basis for deciding which topics are the determinants of important topics to monitor on social media. Opinion detection on social media has often been used to predict major trends in practice and acceptable organizational standards.

Some authors have found strong links between social media opinions and real-life events [8, 87, 88]. The detection of opinions on social media can be done through several steps: detection, tracking, classification, and verification—especially in a crisis involving rumors, such as bombing alerts and cyber crises [89].

First, one must identify the contributor (i.e., the one who is expressing the opinion). Second, the sentiments they express must be classified. According to the classic positive/negative/neutral approach, this classification highlights two essential aspects: polarization and information. The next step is the representation scale, a numerical determination of an opinion's degree of negativity (−1) or positivity (+1). Finally, it is important to look at the purpose of the opinion: what subjects it deals with, who it is about, and what events it is about [90]. For each text, an opinion can be represented by rhetorical aspects, concepts used, and keywords [72]. These opinions are extracted as algorithms that combine the time at which the opinions were expressed, the average of the opinions on a particular topic, the average subjectivity of each opinion, the standard of positive and negative opinions, and the total number of views [90].

6.1.2 Sentiment analysis

Once opinion detection has been achieved, and the classification is done, managing a crisis through social media should lead to sentiment analysis, which is critical when managing situations such as recovery from natural disasters [91].

Sentiment analysis in social media, especially during a crisis, combines the factual elements in the text with the expression of emotions for an effective evaluation of content produced by both individuals and online communities [92–94]. This analysis combines phrases and keywords [90]. It performs a morphological analysis by determining the nouns and verbs used in each sentence using a software program, according to the following declination: a taxonomy of emotion-related words paired according to their common root. This allows a lexical determination based on verbal forms, for example. It is then essential to contextualize the use of the words [95]. These words may be related to feelings, but what they are meant to express may be different depending on the context and the collective understanding community in which they are used [96]. The root match here is no longer enough. Sentiment detection identifies comments found in texts and blogs and annotates them independently of the main articles to aggregate the sentiments appropriately. Sentiment grammar identifies these and then associates them with relevant targets and the owners of those opinions. Sentiment aggregation combines the scores of each feeling expressed on the networks [97].

To better analyze feelings on social media in a crisis, it is necessary to understand them through the dichotomy of normative and informative elements that govern the formation of an opinion. In the processing of a statement, the normative elements are the socialization of the person, their rank within the group and the group itself, and the acquisition of values through an accumulation of information. This element is therefore linked to the subject [98]. This aspect is seen as being stable and difficult to change because of the exposure to social media content. The informational element is related to the purpose of the exchange. It is more likely that social media users are more flexible in this regard and thus adopt or accept a point of view that is different from the one held (or not) before the social media interaction [72]. Sentiment analysis in social media combines psychological and sociological approaches to understand the building blocks of an individual's behavior and, more importantly, their group attitude. Morphosyntactic labeling is one of the best ways to analyze feelings on social media [99]. It is a process of assigning a part of speech to each word in a sentence. This method is used to retrieve information and clarify ambiguity in what is said on networks, and it is essential in processing information. This process also allows easy classification in terms of the following:

1. Closed grammatical categories with a fixed set of words and a determined function in a language, such as pronouns, prepositions, determiners, and conjunctions

2. Closed class category composed of many words and even invented expressions; here, it is possible to find nouns, verbs, adjectives, and adverbs.

The process consists of finding borders between the implicit forms of the expressions and those belonging to the interacting group's metaculture. Thus, sentiment analysis can be used to identify critical trends during increasing interaction on social networks [100], especially during crises.

Sentiment analysis is necessary during a crisis because it provides insight into the morale of users as well as their perceptions of the attribution dynamic. In crisis management, attribution theory is the one that consists in evaluating who is to blame for the crisis. It goes through the analysis of the threat, the determination of the initial responsibility, and the examination of the intensification factors with two elements in mind: consistency (this type of crisis has happened before) and what distinguishes the crisis from other crises [12]. Depending on the nature of the crisis, the thoughts and perceptions of victims, key players, and the public can increase the accountability of the crisis and damage the reputation of the organizations involved or affected by it. The analysis of social media sentiments in this context offers the opportunity to gauge the perception of those immersed in the heart of this crisis and those closely observing its unfolding. The position of the actors at the front of the scene has an impact on the general interpretation of the evolution of the crisis. There are close links between the attribution of responsibility in a crisis and the post-crisis reputation of an organization [79, 101–104]. One could use social networks by scanning opinions and analyzing sentiments on social networks. It is therefore possible to determine how the crises were perceived by those who experienced them from the front lines.

6.2 Quantitative analysis

This section focuses on the literature that describes the use of data models and statistics to explain the complexity and the links between social media and crisis management.

6.2.1 Network analysis

SNA provides information on how people and institutions function during and after disasters and adapt to hazard settings [105]. SNA is the mapping and measurement of relationships and flows between connected people, groups, organizations, computers, URLs, and other information/knowledge entities in a crisis. The network nodes are the people and groups, whereas the links show the relationships or flow between the nodes. SNA provides a visual and mathematical analysis of human relationships [106]. Organizational network analysis allows one to X-ray an organization and reveals the organizational nervous system that connects everything. The analysis of social ties is a field that has grown in importance from establishing the sociology of information and communication techniques [56].

Network analysis allows mapping conversations on a topic to distinguish network types based on their division, density, and direction [107]. There are two types of network analyses: egos network analysis (EAN) and complete network analysis. The EAN assesses the nodes that shape the relationships between actors in the network, making it possible to highlight the operating radius, the diameter of the node and its centrality, the proximity, and the betweenness interaction [108]. While managing a crisis, this exercise allows us to gauge the scope and, therefore, the capacity of influence of information circulating in the network. One can thus determine the nature of the network from the typology of Smith et al. [46]. The centrality of a node measures its prominence or structural importance in a network. A high centrality score can indicate power, influence, control, or status. Determining which node is the most "central" can help disseminate information more quickly in a network, stop epidemics, protect a network from disruption, and identify suspected terrorists, among other things. Network visualization allows for a series of centrality measures to identify the most influential nodes in a social network.

6.2.2 Netnography

Netnography is the adaptation of ethnographic studies on the behaviors and interactions of people on social media. It allows one to map out the key stakeholders and their behaviors during a crisis. It also helps the CMT to gain a clear understanding of the digital infrastructure involved in the crisis [109]. It provides information visualization critical to essential decision making, such as managing the response to a crisis. The technique was efficiently used in the case of the 2015 earthquake in Nepal to establish platforms of communication and effective collaboration between the officials managing the response to that disaster and the stakeholders (the general population and the victims; [110]). Netnography needs to be developed before the crisis, which allows the CMT to know exactly who to talk to and when as well as to anticipate their potential reaction by updating their frequently asked questions to respond appropriately and provide relief.

6.2.3 Applications for disaster

When it comes to crisis triggered by natural disasters, accurate and quality information is critical to predict, prevent and manage the situation. To manage such a crisis, there are a series of tracked metrics, such as TTR (time to respond); MTBF (mean time before failure); MTTR (mean time to recovery, repair, respond, or resolve); MTTF (mean time to failure); and MTTA (mean time to acknowledge), which can help teams properly implement their response. For extreme events such as natural disasters, it is critical to connecting people in need and dire situations with institutions and people who are willing or able to help. Numerous web applications have helped to achieve that results whether during earthquakes, hurricanes, floods, and snow storms by successfully enabling civilians to use their smartphone to produce data, describing the scene and channeling support [111]. Social media in general and web applications, in particular, have been involved in the short-term return to normalcy (**Table 2**) [117, 118].

Natural disaster	Country	Year	Application	Authors
Hokkaido Earthquake	Japan	2018	K-DiPS	Nakai et al. [112]
Lombok Earthquake	Indonesia	2018	Crowhelp	Rachmah et al. [113]
Gorkha Earthquake	Nepal	2015	Urep	Goda et al. [114]
Haiti Earthquake	Haiti	2010	Ushahidi	Yates & Paquette [115]
Chile Earthquake and Tsunami	Chile	2010	Ushahidi	
Wenchuan Earthquake	China	2008	WebGIS	Huang et al. [116]
Saguenay Floods	Canada	1996	Hazus (web application, not mobile)	Natev & Todorov [107]

Table 2.
Non-exhaustive list of web applications playing a key role during natural disasters as per the corpus.

On top making facilitating the collect data, disaster management apps also render the analysis and the process of these data easier by increasing data visualization thus transforming information (raw data) into intelligence (useful information) that could be used to save lives [119].

With the increased use of mobile technology, researchers dealing with crisis management have been developing applications that could help teams foster their ability to use the metrics mentioned above, enabling them to efficiently report, track, and share information as well as interact with victims during emergency situations [8]. The main advantage of these applications is how they leverage data to integrate them into multiple mobile technology sources, thus increasing victims' contribution to the collective knowledge of the extreme event dynamics and intervention team visualization of the situation. These applications have proven useful for critically matching the needs with available resources at the right moment. In some cases, such as the earthquake in Haiti, interventions started on-site, thanks to applications like Ushahidi, an open-source platform providing insights into events happening in near-real time [115]. Crowdsourcing applications and volunteered geographic information have been used in numerous disasters for preparedness, mitigation, and response purposes (**Figure 3**).

6.2.4 Community response grid

Social media network analysis also clearly allows CMT to understand community response grids (CRGs). CRGs integrate mobile technologies and social media, enabling people on a disaster site to report information and respond to instructions from the intervention team, thus facilitating intervention in large-scale emergencies [120]. According to Wu et al. [121], a CRG is a geographically based sociotechnical network that helps local communities become better prepared for and more resilient to emergencies. Empowered by the Internet and mobile technologies, the system helps local communities establish multichannel emergency communication, report emergencies to officials, receive information from official and community sources, coordinate peer-to-peer assistance, provide emotional support, and build trust.

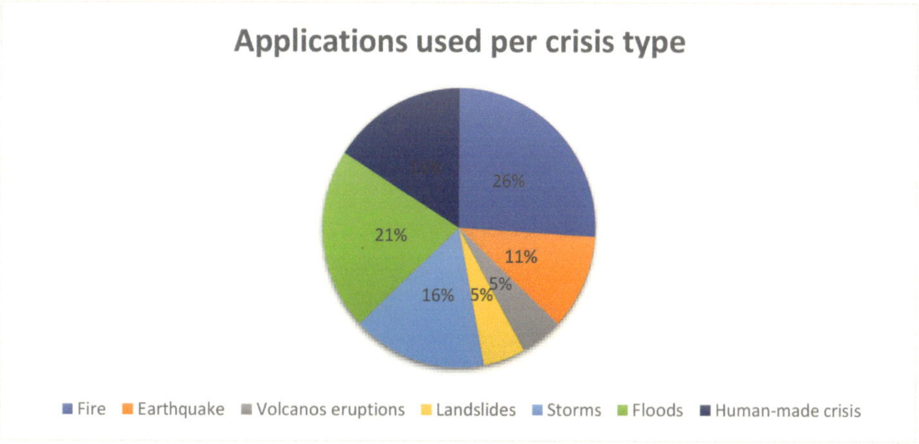

Figure 3.
Breakdown of applications used per crisis type as appeared in the reviewed literature.

7. Conclusion

Social media is incredibly present in people's lives globally. It plays a critical role in managing crises as well. Research has reflected on multidisciplinary approaches to demonstrate the impact of social media on an organization's mitigation, preparedness, readiness, and response and recovery deployment during a crisis. This chapter conducted a systematic literature review assessing how researchers have increasingly used real-life case study models considering related events, precursors, and unperceived variables to understand the governance of uncertainty through social media.

Content analysis focusing on discourse, narratives, videos, and pictures used during a crisis appears to be one of the main methods in the literature to outline social media's influence during a crisis and its use by the crisis management team. Another important method in the domain present in the literature is the network analysis. Here, researchers focus on connectivity and interactivity by analyzing the use of centrality and the importance of nodes during a crisis. The degree of centrality is the most straightforward measure of node connectivity. Sometimes it is helpful to consider degree (number of inbound links) and degree (number of outbound links) as separate measures, for example, when examining transactional data or account activity during a crisis. This method allows the crisis management team to properly channel their responses into action by providing critical information about the most influential actors and subjects. Social media increases the understanding of two crucial elements during a crisis: stakeholders' core needs and concerns. That said, this research has its own limitations. In effect, a crisis can be considered as both danger and opportunity, and social media presents a dangerous opportunity and must be handled with care in times of crisis. With its propensity to spread fake news, misinformation, and rumors, social media can often become a double-edged sword. It can be found at the origin of a crisis and can contribute to amplifying a crisis by amplifying it on a disproportionate scale. This dangerous aspect has not been addressed in this chapter and could become the object of another research project in the future in a holistic attempt to comprehend the main links between crisis management and the use of social media.

Author details

Serge Banyongen
University of Ottawa, Ottawa, Canada

*Address all correspondence to: ebanyong@uottawa.ca

References

[1] Kaplan M, Haenlein A, Haenlein M. Users of the world, unite! The challenges and opportunities of social media. Business Horizons. 2010;**53**:59-68

[2] Earl J, Kimport K. Digital Enabled Social Change: Activism in the Internet Age. Cambridge: MIT Press; 2011. DOI: 10.7551/mitpress/9780262015103.001.0001

[3] Quan-Haase A, Sloan L. Introduction to the handbook of social media research methods: Goals, challenges, and innovations. In: Sloan L, Quan-Haase A, editors. The SAGE Handbook of Social Media Research Methods. London: SAGE Publications Inc.; 2016. pp. 1-9. DOI: 10.4135/9781473983847.n1

[4] Grubmüller V, Götsch K, Krieger B. Social media analytics for future oriented policy making. European Journal of Futures Research. 2013;**1**(1):20. DOI: 10.1007/s40309-013-0020-7

[5] Cheng Y, Spruill T, Dalton C. Social media and crisis communication (SMCC). In: Jin Y, Austin LL, editors. Social Media and Crisis Communication. second ed. New York: Routledge; 2022

[6] Jin Y, Austin LL. Social Media and Crisis Communication. Second ed. New-York: Routledge; 2022. DOI: 10.4324/9781003043409

[7] Yan J, Liu BF, Austin LL. Examining the role of social media in effective crisis management: The effects of crisis origin, information form, and source on publics' crisis responses. Communication Research. 2014;**41**(1):74-94

[8] Saroj A, Pal S. Use of social media in crisis management: A survey. International Journal of Disaster Risk Reduction. 2020;**4**(101584):1-19

[9] Masys AJ. Disaster Forensics: Understanding Root Cause and Complex Causality. Cham, Switzerland: Springer; 2016

[10] Baron G. Response suggestions and public participation are the new norm in response management. Crisis Comm. 2010. Available from: http://www.emergencymgmt.com/emergency-blogs/crisis-comm/Response-Suggestions-and-Public-111510.html

[11] Sweetser KD, Metzgar E. Communicating during the crisis: Use of blogs as a relationship management tool. Public Relations Review. 2007;**33**(3):340-342

[12] Coombs WT. Crisis Communication and Social Media. Essential Knowledge Project; 2008

[13] Wetzstein I, Grubmüller-Régent V, Götsch K, Rainer K. Crisis and social media: A metastudy on pertinent research and practice. Human Technology. 2014;**10**(2):95-124

[14] Vihalemm T, Kiisel M, Harro-Loit H. Citizens' response patterns to warning messages. Journal of Contingencies and Crisis Management. 2012;**20**(1):13-25

[15] Rainer K, Grubmüller V, Pejic I, Götsch K, Leitner P. Social media applications in crisis interaction systems. Connecting Matter, Life, Culture and Technology. 2013;**1**(1):110-127

[16] Špoljarić A. Managing crisis communication via social media. Naše gospodarstvo/Our Economy. 2021;**67**(1):23-32. DOI: 10.2478/ngoe-2021-0003

[17] Bruns A. Crisis communication. In: Cunningham IS, Turnbull S, editors. The Media and Communications in Australia.

Crows Nest, NSW: Allen & Unwin; 2014. pp. 351-355

[18] van der Meer T, Verhoeven P. Public framing organizational crisis situations: Social media versus news media. Public Relations Review. 2013;**39**:229-231

[19] Austin L, Fisher Liu B, Jin Y. How audiences seek out crisis information: Exploring the social-mediated crisis communication model. Journal of Applied Communication Research. 2012;**40**(2):188-207

[20] Fincham K. Exploring political journalism homophily on twitter: A comparative analysis of US and UK elections in 2016 and 2017. Media and Communication. 2019;7(1):213-224

[21] Goolsby R. Social media as crisis platform: The future of community maps/crisis maps. ACM Transactions on Intelligent Systems and Technology (TIST). 2010;**1**(1):1-11. DOI: 10.1145/1858948.1858955

[22] Lee H, Palen A, Palen L. Twitter adoption and use in mass convergence and emergency events. International Journal of Emergency Management. 2009;**6**(3-4):248-260

[23] Backfried G, Göllner J, Quirchmayr G, Rainer K, Kienast G, Thallinger G, et al. Cross-media analysis for communication during natural disasters. Computer and Information Science. 2013;**409**:13-22

[24] Buzoianu C, Bîra M. Using social media listening in crisis communication and management: New methods and practices for looking into crises. Sustainability. 2021, 2021;**13**(23):13015. DOI: 10.3390/su132313015

[25] Jahng MR, Hong S. How should you tweet? The effect of crisis response voices, strategy, and prior brand attitude in social media crisis communication. Corporate Reputation Review. 2017;**20**(2):147-157. DOI: 10.1057/s41299-017-0022-7

[26] Velev D, Zlateva P. In: Lijuan D, editor. Use of Social Media in Natural Disaster Management, International Proceedings of Economics Development and Research. Vol. 39. IACSIT Press; 2012. pp. 41-45. Available from: http://www.ipedr.com/vol39/009-ICITE2012-B00019.pdf [Assessed on December 28th, 2022]

[27] Nilsen LG, Hafstad GS, Staksrud E, Dyb G. Five reasons for using social media among young terror survivors: Results from the Utøya study. Computers in Human Behavior. 2018;**84**:285-294. DOI: 10.1016/j.chb.2018.03.006

[28] Robert M, Stene LE, Garfin DR, Vandentorren S, Motreff Y, du Roscoat E, et al. Media exposure and post-traumatic stress symptoms in the wake of the November 2015 Paris terrorist attacks: A population-based study in France. Frontiers in Psychiatry. 2021;**12**:509457. DOI: 10.3389/fpsyt.2021.509457

[29] Creswell JW, Plano Clark VL. Designing and Conducting Mixed Methods Research. 2nd ed. Los Angeles: Sage Publications Ltd.; 2011

[30] Snelson LC. Qualitative and mixed methods social media research: A review of the literature. The International Journal of Qualitative Methods. 2016;(1):1-15. DOI: 10.1177/16094069156245

[31] Fink A. Conducting Research Literature Reviews: From the Internet to Paper. 4th ed. Thousand Oaks: Sage Publications, Inc; 2010

[32] Rasmussen J, Øyvind I. Risk, crisis, and social media: A systematic review

of seven years' research. Nordicom Review. 2017;**38**(2):1-17. DOI: 10.1515/nor-2017-0393

[33] Kankanamge N, Yigitcanlar T, Goonetilleke A, Kamruzzaman MD. Determining disaster severity through social media analysis: Testing the methodology with south East Queensland flood tweets. International Journal of Disaster Risk Reduction. 2019;**42**:101360. DOI: 10.1016/j.ijdrr.2019.101360

[34] Zhu L, Anagondahalli D, Zhang A. Social media and culture in crisis communication: McDonald's and KFC crises management in China. Public Relations Review. 2017;**43**:487-492

[35] Bundy J, Pfarrer MD, Short CE, Coombs WT. Crises and crisis management: Integration, interpretation, and research development. Journal of Management. 2017;**43**(6):1661-1692

[36] Lai IKW, Wong JWC. Comparing crisis management practices in the hotel industry between initial and pandemic stages of COVID-19. International Journal of Contemporary Hospitality Management. 2020;**32**(10):3135-3156

[37] Boin A, Hart P, Stern E, Sundelius B. The Politics of Crisis Management: Public Leadership under Pressure. Second edition. Cambridge: Cambridge University Press; 2014. DOI: 10.1017/9781316339756

[38] Berger AA. Media and Communication Research Methods: An Introduction to Qualitative and Quantitative Approaches. Third ed. Thousand Oaks: Sage; 2013

[39] Neuendorf KA. The Content Analysis Guidebook. Second ed. SAGE Publications Inc.; 2017

[40] MacKay M, Colangeli T, Gillis D, McWhirter J, Papadopoulos A. Examining social media crisis communication during early COVID-19 from public health and news media for quality, content, and corresponding public sentiment. International Journal of Environmental Research and Public Health. 2021;**18**(15):7986. DOI: 10.3390/ijerph18157986

[41] Warrens MJ. Five ways to look at Cohen's kappa. Journal of Psychology & Psychotherapy. 2015;**5**:197. DOI: 10.4172/2161-0487.1000197

[42] Cameron MA, Power R, Robinson B, Yin J. Emergency situation awareness from twitter for crisis management. In: Proceedings of the 21st International Conference on World Wide Web. Lyon France; 2012. pp. 695-698

[43] Helsloot I, Groenendaal J. Twitter: An underutilized potential during sudden crises. Research note. Journal of Contingencies and Crisis Management. 2013;**21**(3):179-183

[44] Hansen D, Sheiderman B, Smith MA. Analyzing Social Media Networks with NodeXL: Insights from a Connected World. 2nd edition. Cambridge: Morgan Kaufmann; 2010

[45] Pew Research Center, Social Media Foundation. How we analyzed Twitter social media networks with NodeXL. 2014. Available from: http://www.pewinternet.org/files/2014/02/How-we-analyzed-297 Twitter-social-media-networks.pdf page [Assessed: April 14, 2022]

[46] Smith A, Marc Lee Rainie, Ben Shneiderman, ItaiHimelboim. Mapping twitter topic networks: From polarized crowds to community clusters, report, pew research center. 20 February, 2014;**2014**. Available from: https://www.researchgate.net/publication/260478854_Mapping_Twitter_Topic_Networks_From_Polarized_Crowds_to_Community_Clusters

[47] Bruns A, Liang Y. Tools and methods for capturing twitter data during natural disasters. First Monday. 2012;**17**:4-3. DOI: 10.5210/fm.v17i4.3937

[48] Bruns A, Burgess J, Crawford K, Shaw F. #Qldfloods and @QPSMedia: Crisis Communication on Twitter in the 2011 South East Queensland Floods. Brisbane: ARC Centre of Excellence for Creative Industries and Innovation; 2012

[49] Loukouman A. Le marketing des réseaux sociaux. Paris: MA Éditions; 2012

[50] Ki E-J, Nekmat E. Situational crisis communication and interactivity: Usage and effectiveness of Facebook for crisis management by fortune 500 companies. Computers in Human Behavior. 2014;**35**:140-147. DOI: 10.1016/j.chb.2014.02.039

[51] Hagen L, Keller T, Neely S, DePaula N, Robert-Cooperman C. Crisis Communications in the Age of Social Media. Social science computer review. 2018;**36**(5):523-541. DOI: 10.1177/0894439317721985

[52] Kelleher T. Conversational voice, communicated commitment, and public relations outcomes in interactive online communication. Journal of Communication. 2009;**59**(1):172-188. DOI: 10.1111/j.1460-2466.2008.01410.x

[53] Ferguson N. The Square and the Tower. Networks and Power, from the Freemasons to Facebook. New-York: Penguin Books; 2019

[54] Fowler CA, Fowler JH. Connected: The Surprising Power of our Social Networks and How they Shape our Lives—How your friends' friends' Friends Affect Everything you Feel, Think, and Do. New York: Back Bay Books; 2011

[55] Castells M. The Rise of the Network Society. second ed. Chichester, West Sussex; Malden, MA: Willey Blackwell; 2011

[56] Dagiral É, Martin O. Liens sociaux numériques. Sociologie. 2017;**1**(8)

[57] Huisman M, van Duijn MAJ. Software for social network analysis. In: Carrington PJ, Scott J, Wasserman S, editors. Models and Methods in Social Network Analysis. Cambridge, New York: Cambridge University Press; 2005. pp. 270-316

[58] Ferber PH, Pugliese RR. Partisans, proximates, and poker players: The impact of homophily and proximity on communication patterns of state legislators. Polity. 2000;**32**:401-141

[59] Hirsch BT, Suzanne P, Stephanie AH, Stanley DG. Genetic relatedness does not predict racoon social network structure. Animal Behaviour. 2013;**85**(2):463-470. DOI: 10.1016/j.anbehav.2012.12.011

[60] Bischoff K. We love rock "n" roll: Analyzing and predicting friendship links in Last.fm. Presented at the WebSci '12: Proceedings of the 3rd Annual ACM Web Science Conference: 2012. DOI: 10.1145/2380718.2380725

[61] Pariser E. The Filter Bubble: How the New Personalized Web Is Changing What we Read and How we Think. London: Pinguin Editions; 2012

[62] Dahlgren PM. A critical review of filter bubbles and a comparison with selective exposure. Nordicom Review. 2021;**42**(1):15-33. DOI: 10.2478/nor-2021-0002

[63] Nemoto Y, Klyuev V. Tool to retrieve less-filtered information from the internet. Information. Basel: MDPI AG. 2021;**12**:65. DOI: 10.3390/info12020065

[64] Törnberg P. Echo chambers and viral misinformation: Modeling fake news as complex contagion. PLoS One. 2018;**13**(9):e0203958. DOI: 10.1371/journal.plsone.0203958

[65] Huyghe FB. Fake news, la grande peur. Versailles: VA Press; 2018

[66] Cinelli M, Quattrociocchi W, Galeazzi A, Valensise CM, Brugnoli E, Schmidt AL, et al. The COVID-19 social media infodemic. Scientific Reports. 2020;**10**:05004

[67] Li Z, Qiu H, Zhou Q. Social-mediated diffusion of conspiracy theories about COVID-19: A study integrating SMCC and TPB models. International Journal of Human–Computer Interaction. 2022;**38**(7):680-689

[68] Scannell D, Desens L, Guadagno M, Tra Y, Acker E, Sheridan K, et al. COVID-19 vaccine discourse on twitter: A content analysis of persuasion techniques, sentiment, and mis/disinformation. Journal of Health Communication. International Perspectives. 2021;**26**(7):443-459

[69] Wen-Ying S, Budenz A. Considering emotion in COVID-19 vaccine communication: Addressing vaccine hesitancy and fostering vaccine confidence. Health Communication. 2021;**35**(14):1718-1722

[70] Metcalfe B. Metcalfe's law after 40 years of Ethernet. IEEE Computer. 2013;**46**(12):26-31. DOI: 10.1109/MC.2013.374

[71] Huberman AB, Romero DM, Wu F. Social networks that matter: Twitter under the microscope. First Monday. 2009;**14**(1):1-9

[72] Sobkowicz P, Kaschesky M, Bouchard G. Opinion mining in social media: Modeling, simulating, and forecasting political opinions in the web. Government Information Quarterly. 2012;**29**(4):470-479

[73] Yang M, Kiang M, Ku Y, Chiu C, Li Y. Social media analytics for radical opinion mining in hate group web forums. Journal of Homeland Security and Emergency Management. 2011;**8**(1):1-17

[74] Campbell C, Pitt LF, Parent M, Berthon P. Tracking back-talk in consumer-generated advertising. Journal of Advertising Research. 2011;**51**(1):224-238

[75] Bengston DN, Fan DP, Reed P, Goldhor-Wilcock A. Rapid issue tracking: A method for taking the pulse of the public discussion of environmental policy. Environmental Communication. 2009;**3**(3):367-385

[76] Ruggiero A, Marita V. Social media monitoring for crisis communication: Process, methods, and trends in the scientific literature. Online Journal of Communication and Media Technologies. 2014;**4**(1):105-130

[77] Rappaport SD. Listening solutions. Journal of Advertising Research. 2010;**50**(2):197-213. DOI: 10.2501/S00218491009135X

[78] Coombs WT, Holladay JS. Unpacking the halo effect: Reputation and crisis management. Journal of Communication Management. 2006;**10**(2):123-137

[79] Coombs WT, Holladay JS. The paracrisis: The challenges created by publicly managing crisis prevention. Public Relations Review. 2012;**38**(3):408-415

[80] Karafillakis E, Martin S, Simas C, Olsson K, Takacs J, Dada S, et al. Methods for social media monitoring related to

vaccination: Systematic scoping review. JMIR Public Health and Surveillance. 2021;7(2):e17149. DOI: 10.2196/17149

[81] Ebner J, Chris K, Harvey W. Is there a language of terrorists? a comparative manifesto analysis. Studies in Conflict & Terrorism. 2022;**45**(12):1-12. DOI: 10.1080/1057610X.2022.2109244

[82] Liu F, Xu D. Social roles and consequences in using social media in disasters: A structurational perspective. Information Systems Frontiers. 2018;**20**(4):693-711. DOI: 10.1007/s10796-017-9787-6

[83] Zeng D, Chen H, Lusch R, Li S. Social media analytics and intelligence. IEEE Intelligent Systems. 2010;**25**(6):13-16

[84] Stieglitz S, Dang-Xuan L. Social media and political communication: A social media analytics framework. Social Network Analysis and Mining. 2013;**3**:1277-1291

[85] Larson K, Watson RT. The value of social media: Toward measuring social media strategies. Paper presented at the 32nd International Conference on Information Systems (ICIS). Shanghai, China; 2011

[86] Macnamara J. New insights into crisis communication from an "inside" emic perspective during COVID-19. Public Relations Inquiry. 2021;**10**(2):237-262

[87] Kramer AD. An unobtrusive behavioral model of "gross national happiness." [conference presentation]. In: SIGCHI Conference on Human Factors in Computing Systems, Atlanta, GA, USA. New York, NY, USA: Association for Computing Machinery; 2010. pp. 287-290

[88] Thelwall M, Buckley K, Paltoglou G. Sentiment in twitter events. Journal of the American Society for Information Science and Technology. 2011;**62**:406-418

[89] Zubiaga A, Aker A, Bontcheva K, Liakata M, Procter R. Detection and resolution of rumours in social media: A survey. ACM Computing Surveys. 2018;**51**(2):1-32

[90] Maynard D, Gerhard G, Funk A, Fisichella M. Should I care about your opinion? Detection of opinion interestingness and dynamics in social media. Future Internet. 2014;**6**:457-481

[91] Beigi G, Hu X, Maciejewski R, Liu H. An overview of sentiment analysis in social media and its applications in disaster relief. In: Pedrycz W, Chen SM, editors. Sentiment Analysis and Ontology Engineering. Studies in Computational Intelligence. Vol. 639. Cham: Springer; 2016. DOI: 10.1007/978-3-319-30319-2_13

[92] Chmiel A, Sienkiewicz J, Thelwall M, Paltoglou G, Buckley K, Kappas A, et al. Collective emotions online and their influence on community life. PLoS One. 2011;**6**:e22207

[93] Sobkowicz P, Sobkowicz A. Two-year study of emotion and communication patterns in a highly polarized political discussion forum. Social Science Computer Review. 2012;**30**(4):448-469. DOI: 10.1177/0894439312436512

[94] Ding F, Liu Y. Modeling opinion interactions in a BBS community, The European Physical Journal B. 2010;**78**:245-252. DOI: 10.1140/epjb/e2010-10453-9

[95] Öztürk N, Ayvaz S. Sentiment analysis on twitter: A text mining approach to the Syrian refugee crisis. Telematics and Informatics. 2018;**35**(1):136-147. DOI: 10.1016/j.tele.2017.10.006

[96] Fersini E. Sentiment analysis in social networks: A machine learning perspective. In: Pozzi FA, Fersini E, Messina E, Liu B, editors. Sentiment Analysis in Social Networks. Cambridge, MA: Morgan Kaufmann; 2017. pp. 91-111

[97] Kaur HJ, Kumar R. Sentiment analysis from social media in crisis situations. International Conference on Computing, Communication & Automation. 2015:251-256. DOI: 10.1109/CCAA.2015.7148383

[98] Banyongen S. Terrorisme et communication de crise. Paris: Connaissances et Savoirs; 2016

[99] Liu Bing. Web Data Mining: Exploring Hyperlinks, Contents, and Usage Data. Berlin: Springer; 2011

[100] Stieglitz S, Dang-Xuan L, Burns A, Neuberger C. Social media analytics: An interdisciplinary approach and its implications for information systems. Business & Information Systems Engineering. 2014;**2**:89-96

[101] Coombs WT, Holladay JS. Communication and attributions in a crisis: An experimental study of crisis communication. Journal of Public Relations Research. 1996;**8**(4):279-295

[102] Coombs WT, Holladay JS. An extended examination of the crisis situation: A fusion of the relational management and symbolic approaches. Journal of Public Relations Research. 2001;**13**:321-340

[103] Coombs WT, Holladay JS. Helping crisis managers protect reputational assets: Initial tests of the situational crisis communication theory. Management Communication Quarterly. 2002;**16**:165-186

[104] Coombs WT, Schmidt L. An empirical analysis of image restoration: Texaco's racism crisis. Journal of Public Relations Research. 2000;**12**(2):163-178

[105] Jones E, Faas AJ, editors. Social Network Analysis of Disaster Response, Recovery, and Adaptation. Kidlington, Oxford: Elsevier Science & Technology; 2016

[106] Romascanu A, Ker H, Sieber R, Greenidge S, Lumley S, Bush D, et al. Using deep learning and social network analysis to understand and manage extreme flooding. Special Issue: Knowledge, Semantics and AI for Risk and Crisis Management. 2020;**28**(3):251-261

[107] Miroslav N, Todorov N. Hazus: A standardized methodology for flood risk assessment in Canada. Canadian Water Resources Journal/Revue canadienne des ressources hydriques. 2013;**38**(3):223-231. DOI: 10.1080/07011784.2013.801599

[108] Oggier F, Datta A, Phetsouvanh S. An ego network analysis of sextortionists. Social Network Analysis and Mining. 2020;**10**:44. DOI: 10.1007/s13278-020-00650-x

[109] Hoejgaard CD. Dealing with the Platform: The Role of Affordances in Netnography as Rapid Research. SAGE Research Methods; 2022. DOI: 10.4135/9781529600445

[110] Subba R, Tung B. Online convergence behavior, social media communications and crisis response: An empirical study of the 2015 Nepal earthquake police twitter project. In: Proceedings of the 50th Hawaii International Conference on System Sciences. Hilton Waikoloa Village, Hawaii; 2017

[111] Goncalves A, Silva C, Morreale P, Bonafide J. Crowdsourcing for public safety. IEEE International Systems Conference Proceedings. 2014;**2014**:50-56. DOI: 10.1109/SysCon.2014.6819235

[112] Nakai H, Itatani T, Horiike R. Application software that can prepare for disasters based on patient-participatory evidence: K-DiPS: A verification report. International Journal of Environmental Research and Public Health. 2022;**19**:9694. DOI: 10.3390/ijerph19159694

[113] Ida R, Gunawan E, Widiyantoro S, Sunarti E, Indah G, Marliyani, et al. Social networks and local communication network patterns following the destructive 2018 Lombok. Indonesia, earthquake sequence, Geomatics, Natural Hazards and Risk. 2022;**13**(1):451-473. DOI: 10.1080/19475705.2022.2033854

[114] Goda K, Kiyota T, Pokhrel RM, Chiaro G, Katagiri T, Sharma K, et al. The 2015 Gorkha Nepal earthquake: Insights from earthquake damage survey. Frontiers in Built Environment. 2015;**1**:8. DOI: 10.3389/fbuil.2015.00008

[115] Yates D, Paquette S. Emergency knowledge management and social media technologies: A case study of the 2010 Haitian earthquake. International Journal of Information Management. 2011;**31**(1):6-13

[116] Huang Y, Hung Wong. Effects of social group work with survivors of the Wenchuan earthquake in a transitional community. Health and Social Care. 2012;**21**(3):327-337. DOI: 10.1111/hsc.12022

[117] Ogie RI, James S, Moore A, Dilworth T, Amirghasemi M, Whittaker J. Social media use in disaster recovery: A systematic literature review. International Journal of Disaster Risk Reduction. 2022;**70**(2022):102783

[118] Huang R, Huang R, Ju JHN, Li W. WebGIS-based information management system for landslides triggered by Wenchuan earthquake. Natural Hazards. 2012;**65**(3):1507-1517

[119] Jason K, Jishnu V, Remya G. Web application for disaster management. International Journal of Advanced Research in Computer and Communication Engineering. 2019;**8**(2):293-296

[120] Jaeger PT, Fleischmann KR, Preece J, Shneiderman B, Wu PF, Qu Y. Community response grids: Using information technology to help communities respond to bioterror emergencies. Biosecurity and Bioterrorism. 2007;**5**(4):335-345. DOI: 10.1089/bsp.2007.0034

[121] Wu PF, Qu Y, Preece J, Shbeiderman B. Community response grid (CRG) for a university campus: Design requirements and implications. [conference presentation]. In: Fiedrich F, Van de Walle B, editors. Proceedings of the 5th International ISCRAM Conference. Washington, DC, USA; 2008

Chapter 2

Revisiting Crisis Governance: Toward Collaborative Crisis Management

Gabriel Lele

Abstract

This chapter attends to three main modes of crisis governance: centralization, decentralization, and collaborative crisis management (CCM). While the first two modes focus almost exclusively on government actors, CCM goes beyond them by involving private sectors and civil society. CCM is a more robust form of crisis governance since it combines knowledge and resources from multiple actors, which is a key to managing the more complex nature of modern crises. This chapter uses the case of Indonesia in dealing with the COVID-19 pandemic to show the dynamics of crisis governance. Indonesia moved from a centralized mode of crisis governance toward a more decentralized one. Simultaneously, there were several collaborative initiatives involving multiple stakeholders to deal with the crisis, such as in the case of SONJO. The case illustrates that while CCM provides a more effective response, it has some limitations as it has a smaller scale, may create internal conflict, lacks sustainability, and has a nonbinding character. The experience of Indonesia lends the lesson that for CCM to be robust crisis governance, and there needs to be a clear arrangement to boost its scale, manage internal conflict, improve sustainability, and induce a more permanent and binding framework.

Keywords: crisis governance, decentralization, centralization, collaboration, COVID-19, SONJO

1. Introduction

As the world is moving toward its more sophisticated version, numerous crises have become the order of the day. Crises have presented the world with their challenging nature, be they natural or man-made. The most current incidence of the COVID-19 pandemic has attracted both academia and practitioners to present a more solid response, and this begins with finding the most appropriate—if not the best—mode of crisis governance [1].

In developing the mode of crisis governance, scholars are divided into two camps. One camp argues that as a crisis requires prompt and decisive responses, a centralized mode of governance is preferable [2, 3]. The opposing camp contends that crisis has multiple causes and effects, necessitating a more localized, contextual response and, as a result, a more decentralized mode of governance [4, 5].

Moving beyond these dichotomous debates, some argue that the choice of governance mode depends highly on contextual, situational, and institutional factors [6, 7]. Some crises, such as wars and economic crises, are better dealt with centralized governance; others, such as pandemics, are better dealt with a more decentralized mode of governance; and still others use a combination of both.

This chapter extends the debates by presenting the third mode of governance, namely collaborative crisis management (hereinafter CCM). CCM refers to an arrangement where multiple stakeholders from different sectors and backgrounds work together to manage a crisis [8, 9]. It argues that, as a crisis brings multiple challenges, involving more stakeholders, including nongovernmental actors with different responsibilities and resources, presents an alternative mode. However, for CCM to be effective, there needs to be a clear arrangement of responsibilities and interactions among these multiple actors.

To pursue this argument, this chapter reviews the existing literature on crisis governance, focusing on the debates among different camps of scholars. Focusing on CCM, it employs the case of Indonesia in dealing with the COVID-19 pandemic. The case was chosen since Indonesia represents a complex institutional choice where it has initially applied centralized governance and then moved toward more decentralized management. In the latter episodes of the pandemic, Indonesia turns to nongovernment actors for more collaboration. The effective work of CCM is illustrated by the case of SONJO. SONJO stands for *Sambatan Jogya,* a Javanese culture that emphasizes solidarity, collaboration, and mutual support. It is a bottom-up approach to dealing with the pandemic, focusing on vulnerable and high-risk societal groups most affected by the pandemic. It uses several WhatsApp groups to accomplish the mission by distributing information on the community's health condition, distributing health and food supplies, promoting small and medium-scale enterprises (SMEs) through online platforms, and initiating vaccine provision for the low-income and rural communities.

This chapter employs a qualitative documentary study by using both primary and secondary documents from various sources [10]. These documents are used in a reflexive process to uncover the moral and political underpinnings behind the text [11]. It assesses government policy documents in responding to and dealing with the pandemic as well as previous research on the same topic. The focus of the analysis is on the dynamics of the choice of crisis governance. In illustrating the case of SONJO, it uses various publications and especially discussions in various WhatsApp groups under SONJO, where the author has been an active member.

This chapter is organized as follows: the following section starts by presenting the theoretical foundation by elaborating on the literature on centralization, decentralization, and CCM. It assesses the advantages and disadvantages of each crisis governance mode. It then discusses the case of Indonesia in responding to the COVID-19 pandemic, which moves from highly centralized governance toward a more decentralized mode. It then presents the case of SONJO to illustrate the move toward more collaborative crisis governance. This chapter concludes with some drawn lessons and implications.

2. Crisis governance in perspective

2.1 Decentralization-centralization debate

Crisis governance has attracted academic enterprises for decades. As the world is moving toward a more sophisticated version, crises have become part of daily life, from war to economic downturn, from pandemic to natural disaster. A crisis is a critical juncture with consequential and far-reaching effects on both institutions and societies [12].

Crises are always associated with events involving complex policy choices and tricky political and ethical dilemmas. This is because crises deal with situations where "cherished national, organizational, and personal values are at stake" ([13], p. 3). As a result, crises can jeopardize a society's high-priority goals, present time constraints and pressure, and surprise the society. That is also why crises always contain not only uncertainty but also urgency and a threat to certain basic values. They create ambiguity and risk, which require prompt, critical, and potentially irreversible decisions ([14], p. 158). While some crises are natural and technical, their management requires a much more complex social and political process, which may lead to institutional complexity or even paralysis.

The institutional complexity posed by a crisis deserves further elaboration as it dictates whether a crisis can be managed well or creates further complications. This institutional complexity has both a horizontal dimension that concerns numerous agencies at the same level of government and a vertical dimension that covers different actors from different levels of government [9]. To these two dimensions, it is also important to add the third dimension, namely the diagonal dimension, dealing with the involvement of nongovernment actors across sectors. As crises have become more complex and given the limited capacities of the government to deal with them, it has become increasingly important to involve actors from all backgrounds. Therefore, the whole-of-government approach must be transformed into the whole-of-nation approach [15].

Even with such a relaxation of the unitary assumption of the state, one must realize that as the world is moving toward more globalized interaction, crises also contain a global (not only domestic) dimension. This implies that crises beg attention to the international aspect, where global actors, values, and preferences may come together or clash. Therefore, the management of certain crises on a global scale must also consider such global dynamics. Even the traditional approach to the studies of epidemics and pandemics, for example, has come to realize the importance of the global context as they are restricted within and by national boundaries [16].

This discussion sets the background for the importance of understanding crisis governance. Reliable crisis governance will provide credible warnings and forecasts and emergency responses once a crisis develops [1, 17, 18]. Credibility is explained by differing institutional contexts and governance structures among countries [19].

Departing from the institutional approach, crisis governance is divided into two main camps: centralization and decentralization.[1] The choice of either camp has spurred a lasting debate concerning its workability in ensuring efficient communication and coordination, which are key to successfully dealing with a crisis [21].

2.1.1 Centralization mode

The centralization mode aspires to a more command-and-control governance where the decision-making process centers on one specific point only. This might refer to the national government where a specific body of crisis management is

[1] There are two other ways of categorizing crisis governance modes: responsive versus responsible governance and stiff versus flexible governance [20]. The author uses decentralization versus centralization modes as it is the most debated category in crisis literature.

responsible for making the decision and monitoring its implementation. It could also manifest in the domination of the government over nongovernment actors. The other form is when political deliberation gives way to the technocratic process by, for example, constraining, undermining, or even bypassing the parliament's scrutiny and legislative power [22]. The implementation of that decision could be either centralized or decentralized.

The centralization mode is argued to work better for decisive and prompt decisions in responding to a crisis where the cost of delay is high [4, 23]. Goetz [20], for example, shows that the need for action by the national government sometimes contradicts the time-consuming nature of democratic deliberation and therefore requires a much simpler and concentric arrangement. At worst, democracy may compromise the effective response and management of certain crises, such as nuclear leakage or natural disasters. These types of crises are better left to those with expertise, seniority, and experience, leading to only a limited number of leaders, and they may override the claims of democracy [14].

Wang and Wang [23] also argue that as a crisis may bring together different institutions with different preferences and priorities, leading to complex multisector cooperation, a special and centralized chain of command is required to coordinate a joint response. This line of reasoning is consistent with Tsebelis' [24] claim that more concentric governance, i.e., fewer veto players, leads to decisive policy. Centralized governance creates a clear point of accountability, and this provides an institutional incentive for a more responsive polity. When one specific unit in a polity is responsible for managing a crisis, the pressure for performance is strong since people can easily identify where to point their finger for either fame or shame. The pressure serves as an incentive for the unit to perform its best, resulting in good policy delivery.

The presence of a centralized body also enables a clear and well-coordinated release of information for the public, not to create further complications, uncertainty, and stress [25]. Under crisis circumstances, valid and credible information is critical. Information may come from different sources, but only one single institution must be responsible for managing and disclosing such information. Jin et al. [26] maintain that under crisis, effective information communication is critical as the public has many alternative sources of information due to the development of social media. This development may (mis) lead to different reactions and policy directions unless crisis communication professionals can address it. Moreover, as many polities tend to employ a multidisciplinary crisis management team to present a more comprehensive response [27], centralized control is needed.

For the sake of efficient decision-making and when there is a lack of trust in the locals, centralization is also preferable [4]. The issue of local trust is important as there is always tension between the national and subnational governments in both unitary and federal states. Mishra [28] introduces four dimensions of trust, namely competence, openness, concern, and reliability. These components are argued to be negatively correlated to centralization of decision-making, undistorted communication, and collaboration within and between organizations during a crisis.

Despite its merits, the centralization mode is broadly criticized for its limitations. One criticism focuses on the danger it puts on democratic governance. Some crises are so complicated that public participation concerning information and resource sharing is critical. Moreover, since centralization frequently bypasses the political process, it is deemed a nondemocratic mode that leads to a legitimacy crisis, or what Maatsch and Cooper [22] dubbed "governance without democracy." Goetz [20] also maintains

DOI: http://dx.doi.org/10.5772/intechopen.106129

that concentration of authority due to urgency runs the risk of policy and political legitimacy. Against the liberal democratic view of democracy, the civic-republican tradition calls for a more democratic decision-making process, which manifests itself in the issue of participation, inclusion, and deliberation [29]. Therefore, the need for a rapid response must be arranged in such a way as not to time-out democratic procedures while keeping pace with such rapid development [30].

A unified and centralized mode of governance is deemed susceptible to error or even abuse of power. Reflecting on the case of Chinese crisis governance, Bardhan [31] raises his concern for such a risk as centralized governance lacks sufficient downward (and horizontal) accountability and there is no sufficient mechanism for scrutiny and checks. The polities with this system are prone to overreaction to a crisis and therefore less resilient. These criticisms give way to the development of the second camp, which aspires to a more decentralized mode of crisis governance.

2.1.2 Decentralization mode

The decentralization mode argues that it promises better adaptation, a stronger division of responsibility, and enhanced room for innovation [4, 7]. Certain types of crisis, especially ones of local magnitude, require adaptation or contextualization. Decentralization enables such adaptation, through which, crisis responses adjust to local conditions, utilize local knowledge, and maximize local potential.

Decentralized crisis governance can also provide a strong avenue for coordination, provided that there is a free flow of communication among actors [21]. The reason why coordination is difficult under decentralized governance is because of the self-centered orientation among actors, but this can be addressed by developing several channels of communication. This communication will reduce uncertainty as each actor may internalize the risk his/her decision poses to others. When information is important and uncertainty is high, as is typical in many crisis circumstances, actors will communicate more. As a result, decentralization does not have to mean sacrificing a quick and decisive policymaking process. On the contrary, it improves the quality of the policymaking process on the one hand and enhances effective policy implementation on the other hand, making decentralized governance a key benefit for effectively dealing with crises. Under such an arrangement, the central unit may still exist, but it functions more as an information aggregator and communicator.

Decentralized crisis governance also has the benefit of putting the control of crisis management in the hands of those closest to society. Following the subsidiarity or delegation principle, the local managers assume more responsibility, a sense of crisis, and the capacity to adapt to new developments [7]. As they are front-liners, working closely and directly with the people, they are under constant pressure to perform their best. This requires discretion and flexibility as well, and decentralization provides just that [32]. The opposite is also true: local managers are highly frustrated when confronted with pressing issues such as crises right in front of them without sufficient power delegation. This may lead to strategic evasion when actors are pointing fingers at each other in an unfriendly situation [33].

Finally, decentralized crisis governance is preferable when there is strong organizational commitment. As discussed previously, centralization is frequently triggered by—and triggers—distrust. When there is a strong commitment toward a common goal that leads to mutual trust, decentralization may prevail [34]. The other situation would be when there is visionary leadership and active citizenry [35].

These dichotomous perspectives have still provoked lasting debates among scholars. One of the immediate outcomes of such debates is the development of a new perspective trying to combine both perspectives. The two perspectives are not mutually exclusive, and they have both advantages and disadvantages [34]. Hlepas [35], for example, maintains that crisis governance, just like many other types of governance, must be able to strike a balance between responsiveness and responsibility, between democratic legitimacy and social acceptability. Crises indeed require a prompt and decisive response. However, given its irreversible nature, there has to be a mechanism to ensure the quality of the response, and this may lead to the need for more consultation or participation. Moreover, participation and decisive response may go together and are mutually reinforcing. This progression resulted in the introduction of a third approach known as "collaborative crisis management," "joint crisis management," or simply partnership. The following section will discuss this approach.

2.2 Toward collaborative crisis governance

Reflecting on the merits and perils of both centralized and decentralized modes of crisis governance, some experts called for a complementary, if not a supplementary, mode of crisis management. Simply defined, CCM is "the joint efforts of multiple autonomous actors to work across organizational borders, levels of authority, and sectors to prepare for, respond to, and learn from risks and extreme events that disrupt our modern society" ([8], p. 1). It refers to "the collective efforts of multiple autonomous actors working across organizational boundaries, levels of authority, and sectors to prepare for, respond to, and learn from risks and extreme events that disrupt our modern society" ([9], p. 512). This implies an integration of knowledge, information, and experiences, which are then transformed into collective actions.

The introduction of CCM is in line with the development of an enormous literature on collaborative governance. Defined as an administrative or political arrangement that directly and actively engages non-state actors, especially in a collective decision-making process based on the principles of consensus and deliberation to achieve specific collective goals [36], collaborative governance has been introduced extensively on many policy fronts at local, national, and global levels. The new arrangement is deemed important not only for technical purposes but also for more fundamental goals that deal with the principles of democracy. Collaboration, at the very least, increases policy, government, and state legitimacy [37]. CCM is then a mix of collaborative public management and crisis management [38].

CCM comes in different manifestations. One would be where several national government agencies form a joint crisis management unit, normally by putting their representatives into an ad hoc or permanent body. The second form would be the establishment of a joint unit consisting of both national and subnational representatives or where different levels of government are assigned different types of responsibilities. This type of CCM is known as concurrency [17]. The last type of CCM is the involvement of various government and nongovernment actors from different backgrounds in a loosely knit, function-based arrangement. They may have different types and degrees of contribution, but all are oriented toward the same goals. In some cases, as crises move beyond national jurisdiction, a collaborative arrangement at the regional or global level is sometimes called for, implying a regional or global collaborative crisis management [7].

The introduction of collaborative crisis management is in line with the nature of crises and the development of modern society in general. Bynander and Nohrstedt ([8], p. 1) maintain that modern society is facing complex and uncertain risks and hazards and that there needs to be an institutional arrangement and governance approach that "enables flexible solutions and responses based on capacities to innovate, improvise, and adapt to rapidly changing circumstances and complex problems." They call for the "mobilization of more diverse networks of organizations that pool different mandates, resources, skills, and capabilities," something the traditional hierarchical bureaucracy cannot do. This implies a paradigm shift from a simple dichotomous approach of decentralized-centralized arrangement to a more complex arrangement. Moreover, crises are sometimes too complex to be managed by one single actor. Therefore, managing crises in an increasingly complex world requires a radical shift from the whole-of-government or whole-of-society paradigm toward the whole-of-nation paradigm [15].

In its application, CCM may come in different forms. The ideal situation is one in which all stakeholders from the government, private sector, and civil society collaborate in formal or mostly informal arrangements. In several cases, the government only collaborates with the private sector because it has more resources, such as supplies, and the capacity to produce better results [39, 40]. The last form of CCM is when the government collaborates with civil society actors such as NGOs. They work closely and more effectively with the most vulnerable groups, as they have a strong line of communication and respect, which can reduce distrust [41]. Civil society can also coproduce responses to a crisis, either directly by supplying needed resources or by simply complying with crisis countermeasures [42].

Popular as it is, CCM requires careful arrangement as there are several points of concern. A more collaborative mode of crisis governance must also be arranged in such a way as to avoid a strong disposition toward a joint decision trap or institutional rigidity [12]. Bringing more people implies more views and interests, and they may run against each other. If such a propensity cannot be managed effectively, then institutional paralysis—or at least policy paralysis—may develop. This concern has become the subject of intricate debates among scholars. Parker and Sundelius [9], for example, maintain that despite its popularity, collaborative crisis management needs to address five common failures: imagination, initiative, coordination and cooperation, credibility, and learning. To avoid this, there has to be "the mobilization of critical knowledge and scientific advice to improve planning, training, preparedness, capacity building, and, when needed, the effective management of crises."

A similar concern is also raised by Larsson [43]. He maintains that the emergence and presence of collaborative crisis management networks involving public and private actors imply a major managerial challenge for public authorities. In a formal sense, public authorities must initiate and maintain various organizational architectures and technical systems to facilitate functional collaboration in loosely and temporarily composed arrangements. The collaborating actors from different backgrounds must communicate effectively to reach an informed decision under pressing and uncertain conditions. He argues that for a collaborative crisis arrangement to be effective, managers or people in charge must attend closely to the nature of relationships and the potential deadlocks of such a system.

To address this concern, CCM requires strong and effective leadership as it must bring together different, sometimes opposing, views and interests into a single direction [44]. There is ample evidence that the lack of leadership led to poor crisis handling, which caused loss of life and property [45, 46]. Using the case of Turkey, Kapucu and Ustun [47] show that core leadership competencies have a significant effect on the effectiveness of crisis management. They categorized leadership competencies into three types—task-oriented, people-oriented, and organization-oriented—and found that task-oriented competencies have the most significant positive effect on the effectiveness of crisis leadership. This deals with the problem-solving and innovation and creativity management competencies. The other types of competencies have more moderate yet positive effects.

Moving beyond leadership and other technical or managerial concerns, CCM needs to be approached critically. Persson and Granberg [38] expressed concern about the scope of collaboration, which they believe will limit its capacity. Cristofoli et al. [48] maintain the importance of legitimacy and accountability. Similarly, Parker and Sendelius [9] revisited core assumptions of CCM by focusing on several areas such as starting points, level of collaboration, goal formulation, adaptation, involvement, role of non-state actors, and the prevalence and impact of political fighting. For example, whether a crisis management unit should rely strictly on previous arrangements with familiar partners or whether a new scheme of collaboration should be introduced to involve more partners. This deals with the question of the stability and flexibility of CCM, and the answer to this question may be contingent upon the type and scale of the crisis. Also important is whether a CCM adopts a bottom-up or a top-down process. There is also a question of the nature of non-state actor involvement, should it be formally institutionalized or be arranged informally on an ad hoc basis? The most intricate question is political infighting. As crises create tension, conflict among collaborators may emerge, and there needs to be a ready mechanism for conflict resolution and management, such as a conflict management plan, clear participation channels, and transparency mechanisms. Addressing these and other questions is key to effective collaborative crisis management. The authors remind us that while crisis management requires certainty and stability, there is also a need for adaptation, adjustment, and innovation. Striking a balance among these values would be a daunting challenge, and this epitomizes effective collaborative crisis management as well.

This section concludes that the crises we are facing now and then are more complex than before. They are more turbulent and characterized by surprising, inconsistent, unpredictable, and uncertain features ([49], p. 949). Dealing with this new, more turbulent problem cannot rely on a predefined plan or system, especially that of bureaucratic mechanisms and some form of adhocracy. Turbulent crises require "cross-border collaboration, public innovation, and, perhaps most importantly, the development of robust governance strategies that facilitate and support adaptive and flexible adjustment and entrepreneurial exploration and the exploitation of emerging options and opportunities" ([49], pp. 949-950). CCM has to be arranged in such a way as to realize robust crisis governance.

3. The case of Indonesia: from centralization to collaboration

To illustrate the move from a dichotomous crisis arrangement to a more collaborative one, this section will use Indonesia's response to the COVID-19 pandemic as a showcase. Indonesia is among the countries most hit by this pandemic. As of May 2022, it had confirmed 6,052,764 confirmed cases, with 156,534 deaths, or 2.6% [50]. Since the first case of COVID-19 was confirmed in March 2020, Indonesia has undertaken several policy changes that reflect the fragility of its crisis governance.

Legally speaking, Indonesia has no specific mechanism for dealing with a crisis. The effective law closest to crisis management is Law 24/2007 on Disaster Countermeasures. The law sets some key principles in disaster management by stipulating the principles of togetherness, synergy, and partnership. The main responsibilities for disaster management rest with the national government and subnational governments. The law also stipulates the role and function of civil society and the private sector, the concrete implementation of which must accord with government policy. While this legal framework aspires to collaborative management, its real implementation confirms the superiority of government.

3.1 From centralization to decentralization

In the initial phase of the Covid-19 pandemic (March 2020), the Indonesian government employed highly centralized pandemic management by establishing the Covid-19 Task Force led by the head of the National Disaster Countermeasure Agency. The agency is responsible for coordinating all other ministries and agencies and, to a very limited extent, provincial governments concerning decision-making and implementation. The arrangement confirms the centralist nature of CCM. By law, this is because of the nature of the pandemic, which is national and even global. This approach has provoked negative regional sentiment and several regions took different measures from what Jakarta decided. When the president declared Covid-19 as a national emergency in late March 2020, there were strong regional calls for the introduction of quarantine or lockdown. However, the president decided to instead implement the large-scale social restriction, arguing that Indonesia has learned from other countries' bitter experiences with quarantine and there has to be room for economic activities and people's mobility. Such preference provoked an even stronger regional opposition and several subnational governments take opposing measures to contain the virus. This is evident in local policy measures such as local lockdown, partial lockdown, and regional quarantine as shown in **Table 1**. This intergovernmental tension pinpoints the institutional root of crisis management paralysis when centralized directives were introduced under a highly decentralized arrangement [51].

The way the government responded to the pandemic in this initial phase has led to public confusion, frustration, and distrust [52]. As the pandemic has spread nationally, there have been strong calls for better and stronger inter-organizational and inter-jurisdictional collaboration [53]. This includes the involvement of the local government in both the decision-making and implementation process. For this reason, the national government changed its policy course. On April 13th, 2020, President Jokowi Widodo made a radical change. After promulgating COVID-19 as a national disaster, he extended the scope of the crisis management response team by incorporating governors, mayors, and regents. The president also ordered the establishment of the COVID-19 Task Force at each level of government. At the same time, the national government developed several guiding principles for subnational governments to follow through on. Through the Minister of Finance, the national government even tightened the conditions for budget disbursement, focusing local spending on the COVID-19 handling. At this stage, the national government introduced a combination of centralized decision-making with decentralized implementation, leading to a concurrent arrangement [17]. The arrangement is partly collaborative in the sense that it involves both national and subnational governments. The arrangement has eased the intergovernmental tension and led to a more effective response than before. There has been no further tension since then, marking more concerted

Initiatives	Meaning	Subnational governments
Temporary lockdown	Closing two main streets to limit citizen activities	Surabaya City
Regional quarantine	Limiting access to and from the city in 19 strategic points	Surabaya City
Regional isolation	Isolating only regions with infected cases	East Java Province
Extended social restriction	Limiting people's mobility to and from Papua by closing the airport and seaport while applying social distancing	Papua Province
Humanitarian isolation	Requesting the citizens to undertake self-isolation by staying at home and limiting travel activities	Bekasi City
Local lockdown	Restricting people's mobility to and from the region	Sorong City Mamberamo Municipality Tasikmalaya Municipality
Semi-lockdown	Closing schools and tourism objects as well as restricting religious activities	Solo City
Full local lockdown	Restricting all incoming and outgoing cars and passengers	Tegal City
Territorial quarantine	Restricting people's mobility to the region by reducing the operation of ships and planes while strictly inspecting cars	Toli-Toli Municipality
Partial lockdown	Restricting people's mobility to and from the infected community	Banda Aceh City
Local isolation	Isolating several villages with infected cases	Magetan Municipality
Cluster isolation	Isolating the infected and patients under supervision in hospitals and isolating people without symptoms in their community	Medan City

Source: Author's analysis from various sources.

Table 1.
Variations in subnational policy responses (March–April 2020).

action and certain policy direction once lost in the initial period of the pandemic. This arrangement holds up to the time when the chapter is written.

While government response to the pandemic has become much more effective as a result of the crisis governance change, many scholars and practitioners deem it insufficient. Some call for a more community-based system. Dewi and Setyaningsih [54] show the importance of government-private sector collaboration in dealing with patient handling. Similarly, Yuda et al. [55] call for the development of a community-based support system to help people, especially vulnerable groups, better cope with the COVID-19 pandemic. Such a call is important, but it is insufficient. Dealing with a crisis of a turbulent type such as COVID-19 requires more collaborative efforts, and though Indonesia has no formal mechanism yet, there are examples to support the call. SONJO is a case in point.

3.2 SONJO: a collaborative arrangement

SONJO—a traditional form of a communal initiative based on Javanese values, which transforms time and labor to counterweigh the dearth of capital—was established on March 24th, 2020, by some NGO activists and academia in Yogyakarta. The reason behind the initiative was the slow and erratic response of the government in the face of rapid COVID spread. The organizers argued that Indonesia cannot rely solely on the government and that additional initiatives are urgently needed. SONJO ran its campaign through simple WhatsApp groups, given the fact that Indonesians spend an average of 3.5 h per day accessing social media on various platforms. Since its establishment, SONJO has had 2300 members from different backgrounds and institutional affiliations—medical doctors, nurses, hospital managers, researchers, academia, NGO activists, religious leaders, public figures, donors, government officers, and army and police officers—spread throughout 29 WhatsApp groups. Each group dealt with different concerns such as care logistics, supporting facilities (ambulances, tents, and self-isolation shelters), empowerment of small and medium-scale enterprises, exports, transportation, vaccination, and even policy. The group also launched a voluntary scheme of social bidding whereby anyone may take part in responding to the needs shared through the groups. For example, when the vaccination program was first launched, SONJO offered vaccine bidding to its members, and the members may have donated some amount of money to purchase the vaccines and distribute them to the most needy groups [56].

SONJO uses integrity, transparency, empathy, and synergy as its working values. This is due to the nature of the initiatives, which are entirely voluntary and rely on Javanese social capital. All information regarding the development of the COVID cases, logistical needs and conditions, and government policy were shared, discussed, and responded to through the groups that linked to different sectors. Some decisions were not binding but rather an offer that is adjustable. Its commitment is to let no one despair. To monitor the progress and plan for further action, a weekly webinar was held, involving resource persons from various backgrounds. The webinar was a platform for information exchange and the formulation of concrete agendas, focusing on practicality and efficiency.

Given the complexity of the crisis and the paucity of government policy responses, SONJO launched several schemes (**Table 2**). In the health aspect, the SONJO Husada provided hospitals with necessary logistics that the government could not provide,

Cluster of activities	Description
SONJO Angkringan	Regular online sharing sessions involving policy makers, politicians, bureaucrats, entrepreneurs, practitioners, NGO activist, and academia, dealing with the effects of the pandemic and how to respond to them
SONJO Husada	Online sharing sessions and response management in health sector covering logistical supplies, referral system, vaccine provision for vulnerable groups, shelter management, death handling, and teleconsultations
SONJO Pangan	Organizing catering services for isolated patients and online food promotion and trading
SONJO Migunani	Supporting and organizing crowdfunding for social protection, online education such as online business tutorials, and food processing, fashion show, and online trading
SONJO Solidarity Journey	Comparative knowledge and experience sharing with global partners

Source: author's analysis from http://sonjo.id.

Table 2.
Summary of SONJO's activities.

assisted innovators to develop new health equipment, arranged for plasma donors, arranged for referral systems across hospitals, undertook collaborative and voluntary fundraising to support shelters and volunteers, offered teleconsultation, launched a pilot project for medical waste management in shelters, handled dead body treatment and funerals, and sponsored mass vaccination. Concerning mass vaccination, the crowdfunding managed to provide 563,085 doses for communities in Yogyakarta and Central Java. The total value of the donation was USD 81,761 [56].

In terms of the economic aspect, the *SONJO Pangan* started by developing a food database containing information on groceries, traditional markets, and restaurants. It also promoted culinary products, especially during the holy month of Ramadhan, followed by promoting hampers on certain occasions. SONJO also promoted wedding and event organizations using the COVID-19 protocol while simultaneously promoting the export of SME products. It also supported the distribution of logistics to patients in shelters by collaborating with traditional merchants. The isolated patients were also provided with catering services. Of these economic initiatives, SONJO Pangan (Food 1 and Food 2) is the most notable one as it offers a digital platform for SME business transactions at the local, regional, and national levels. SMEs' turnover has declined by no less than 70% during the pandemic, so SONJO initiated the platform to boost SMEs' economic resilience and help them survive the pandemic. In total, SONJO connected 726 food-based SMEs, 37 mini markets, 216 traditional markets, and culinary stalls with buyers nationwide [57].

SONJO has received national and international recognition for its performance. At the national level, SONJO was made a best practice for a bottom-up and collaborative initiative with significant impacts. Initially developed in Jogyakarta, SONJO was then replicated by other local governments such as West Java Province, Magelang Municipality, OKU Timur Municipality, and Lingkar Muria Municipality. While SONJO offered limited schemes of crisis management, it illustrates several important lessons. *First*, it manages to bring together multiple actors with various backgrounds, all sharing the same concern about dealing with the pandemic. When the new crisis management system was in place and the pandemic had stabilized, President Jokowi was quoted repeatedly expressing his concern about the importance of building and strengthening collaboration. This includes not only collaboration between levels of government, but also collaboration between government, the private sector, and civil society [58, 59]. He maintained it not only for stronger domestic collaboration but also for better international cooperation. Such insistence is in line with the most current research. Thielsch et al. [60], for example, propose that a crisis such as the COVID-19 pandemic is a very complex emergency that cannot be handled by individuals, an organization, or even a country. Instead, it requires multidisciplinary crisis management teams at different levels and sectors, highlighting the importance of a collaborative arrangement. Experiences from China, for example, reveal that "good governance requires more than an executive capacity based on command-and-control. It is necessary to develop the ability to work with stakeholders outside the bureaucratic system" [61].

SONJO's experience also confirms that multi-actor collaboration can be established informally based on the principles of voluntariness and solidarity. Such an arrangement presumes the presence and functionality of social capital. Most current research shows that social capital contributes positively and significantly to the control of the pandemic, the absence of which will lead to adverse outcomes [62–64]. The remaining concern for such an arrangement is to apply effective management to avoid conflict among actors by, among others, developing incentives, mutual interdependence, and trust [65]. There were some occasions in SONJO when differences among members led to conflict and actions were delayed since each member is an equal partner. The positive side of such conflict, however, is that SONJO can come up with more informed and well-calculated decisions. What sustained SONJO is the presence of trust, transparency, and integrity.

The next lesson is that, while informal collaborative initiatives are important, they have to improve their scale and sustainability. SONJO relies on social solidarity, but it is contingent upon the presence of social capital, which may be absent elsewhere. With such a distinctive feature, a small-scale initiative needs adaptation before it can be replicated elsewhere. There is also a question of sustainability as such an arrangement is ad hoc and short-term [42]. While adhocracy is commonly found under crisis circumstances, it needs careful management to sustain its operation.

The final point we can draw from the SONJO case study is that crisis responses cannot rely solely on the government. Instead, they may be developed or come from the community or civil society's approach, which is more bottom-up. Complementing government initiatives, the bottom-up initiatives confirm the limitation of more top-down intervention in crisis circumstances that fail to invoke genuine public participation, leading to ineffective pandemic responses [66]. However, for a bottom-up approach to be more effective, the government needs to be involved as it will define the scale and legality of such an initiative. This is critical when a legally binding decision or support beyond voluntary initiatives is needed.

4. Concluding remarks

This chapter reviews the existing debates on crisis governance. Current literature points to a decentralized and centralized mode of crisis governance as the two main modes of crisis governance. Both have advantages and disadvantages. Moving beyond this dichotomy, this chapter offers collaborative crisis management as a supplementary, if not an alternative, mode of crisis governance. Collaborative crisis management provides a more effective response to a crisis as it accumulates knowledge and resources from multiple stakeholders.

Using the case of Indonesia in dealing with the COVID-19 pandemic, this chapter illustrates how these modes of crisis governance were used in combination. Indonesia starts with more centralized governance, then moves toward decentralized crisis management. Since the two modes focus exclusively on government sectors with some limitations, more collaborative initiatives develop, with SONJO as the case in point. The case study shows that the collaborative initiative comes informally from the bottom and its members are only loosely connected through functional bases. While presenting significant contributions to crisis management, a bottom-up collaborative initiative such as SONJO has several limitations. It has limited scale, may create internal conflict, lacks sustainability, and has a nonbinding character. The case of Indonesia is not typical, as some scholars have raised similar concerns [38, 48].

While CCM is commonly practiced, there is no single one-fits-all arrangement, and this is explained by the different sociopolitical contexts and capacities. Different countries may have different models of CCM. Dinan et al. [33], for example, identified different crisis systems across European countries in terms of administrative responsibilities, legal frameworks, and operational practices owing to different national contexts and historical experiences. Similarly, reflecting on the experiences of East Asian countries in dealing with the COVID-19 pandemic, Mao [67] proposes three models of collaborative crisis governance: the Chinese-state-led cooperation; South Korea's state-society synergy; and Japan's social voluntary cooperation model. Despite its differences, there is almost a consensus that collaborative crisis management is more preferable than a dichotomous decentralized and centralized arrangement. The remaining concern is to develop a careful arrangement to make it a robust crisis governance system, such as stipulating clear frameworks for the division of roles and responsibilities and relationships among members.

Acknowledgements

The author wishes to extend his gratitude to anonymous reviewers of the early draft of the manuscript.

Conflict of interest

The author declares no conflict of interest.

Author details

Gabriel Lele
Faculty of Social and Political Sciences, Department of Public Policy and Management, Universitas Gadjah Mada, Yogyakarta, Indonesia

*Address all correspondence to: gabriel.lele@ugm.ac.id; gabilel@ugm.ac.id

References

[1] Zuo W, Zhu W, Wang F, Wei J, Bondar A. Exploring the institutional determinants of risk governance: A comparative approach across nations. International Journal of Disaster Risk Reduction. 2017;**24**:135-143

[2] Raudla R, Bur S, Keel K. The effects of crises and European fiscal governance reforms on the budgetary processes on member states. Journal of Common Market Studies. 2019;**58**:740-756

[3] Fabbrini F. The Euro-crisis, EMU and the perils of centralisation. In: Daniele L, Simone P, Cisotta R, editors. Democracy in the EMU in the Aftermath of the Crisis. Cham, Switzerland: Springer; 2017. pp. 121-139

[4] Bakonyi Z. Why do firms centralise their strategic decision-making during crisis? A qualitative study. Journal of Organizational Change Management. 2018;**31**:1191-1205

[5] Holtmann E, Rademacher C. Decentralization of power and of decision-making: An institutional driver for systems change to democracy. Historical Social Research. 2016;**41**:281-298

[6] Douglas S, Ansell C, Parker CF, Sørensen E, Hart PT, Torfing J. Understanding collaboration: Introducing the collaborative governance case databank. Policy and Society. 2020;**39**:495-509

[7] Kuipers S, Boin A, Bossong R, Hegemann H. Building joint crisis management capacity? Comparing civil security systems in 22 European countries. Risk, Hazards & Crisis in Public Policy. 2015;**6**:1-21

[8] Bynander F, Nohrstedt D. Collaborative crisis management: Inter-organizational approaches to extreme events. In: Bynander F, Nohrstedt D, editors. Collaborative Crisis Management: Inter-Organizational Approaches to Extreme Events. New York: Routledge; 2020. pp. 1-12

[9] Parker CF, Sundelius B. Avoiding the failures of collaborative crisis management: Lessons from research and practice. In: Bynander F, Nohrstedt D, editors. Collaborative Crisis Management: Inter-Organizational Approaches to Extreme Events. New York: Routledge; 2020. pp. 119-131

[10] Bailey K. Methods of Social Research. New York: The Free Press; 1994

[11] Ahmed JU. Documentary research method: New dimensions. Indus Journal of Management & Social Sciences. 2010;**4**:1-14

[12] Benz A, Sonnicksen J. Advancing backwards: Why institutional reform of German federalism reinforced joint decision-making. Publius: The Journal of Federalism. 2018;**48**:134-159

[13] Stern EK. Crisis Decision Making: A Cognitive Institutional Approach. Stockholm: Elanders Gotab; 2003

[14] Kouzmin A. Crisis management in crisis? Administrative Theory & Praxis. 2008;**30**:155-183

[15] Hsieh CW, Wang M, Wong NWM, Ho LK. A whole-of-nation approach to COVID-19: Taiwan's national epidemic prevention team. International Political Science Review. 2021;**42**:300-315

[16] Biswas S. The coronavirus pandemic and global governance: The domestic

diffusion of health norms in global health security crises. Jadavpur Journal of International Relations. 2021;**25**:208-234

[17] Lele G. Concurrency as crisis decision-making governance: Lessons from Indonesia's response to the COVID-19 pandemic. Regional & Federal Studies. 2021. DOI: 10.1080/13597566.2021.1960513 [Published online 1st August 2021]

[18] Mintz A, Wayne C. The polythink syndrome and elite group decision-making. Political Psychology. 2016;**37**:13-21

[19] Kuhlmann S, Bouckaert G, Galli D, Reiter R, van Hecke S. Opportunity management of the COVID-19 pandemic: Testing the crisis from a global perspective. International Review of Administrative Sciences. 2021;**87**:497-517

[20] Goetz KH. A question of time: Responsive and responsible democratic politics. West European Politics. 2014;**37**:379-399

[21] Alonso R, Dessein W, Matouschek N. When does coordination require centralization? American Economic Review. 2008;**98**:145-179

[22] Maatsch A, Cooper I. Governance without democracy? Analysing the role of parliaments in European economic governance after the crisis. Parliamentary Affairs. 2017;**70**:645-654

[23] Wang J, Wang Z. Strengths, weaknesses, opportunities and threats (SWOT) analysis of China's prevention and control strategy for the Covid-19 epidemic. International Journal of Environmental Research and Public Health. 2020;**17**:1-18

[24] Tsebelis G. Veto Players: How Political Institutions Work. Princeton: Princeton University Press; 2002

[25] Torales J, O'Higgins M, Castaldelli-Maia JM, Ventriglio A. The outbreak of COVID-19 coronavirus and its impact on global mental health. International Journal of Social Psychiatry. 2020;**66**:317-320

[26] Jin Y, Liu BF, Austin LL. Examining the role of social media in effective crisis management: The effects of crisis origin, information form, and source on publics' crisis responses. Communication Research. 2014;**41**:74-94

[27] Uitdewilligen S, Waller MJ. Information sharing and decision-making in multidisciplinary crisis management teams. Journal of Organizational Behavior. 2019;**39**:731-748

[28] Mishra AK. Organizational responses to crisis: The centrality of trust. In: Kramer RM, Tyler T, editors. Trust in Organizations. Newbury Park, CA: Sage; 1996. pp. 261-287

[29] Isakhan B, Slaughter S. Introduction: Crisis and democracy in the twenty-first century. In: Isakhan B, Slaughter S, editors. Democracy and Crisis: Democratising Governance in the Twenty-First Century. New York: Palgrave Macmillan; 2014. pp. 1-24

[30] Rosa H, Scheuerman WE. High-Speed Society: Social Acceleration, Power and Modernity. Pennsylvania: Pennsylvania State University Press; 2009

[31] Bardhan P. The Chinese governance system: Its strengths and weaknesses in a comparative development perspective. China Economic Review. 2020;**61**:1-6

[32] Savi R, Randma-Liiv T. Decision-making in time of crisis: Cutback management in Estonia. International Review of Administrative Sciences. 2015;**81**:479-497

[33] Dinan W, Ford A, McConnell A, Pyper R. Policy responses to crisis: The case of the UK firefighters' dispute. Policy & Politics. 2006;**34**:307-323

[34] Raudla R, Douglas JW, Randma-Liiv T, Savi R. The impact of fiscal crisis on decision-making processes in European governments: Dynamics of centralization cascade. Public Administration Review. 2015;**75**:842-852

[35] Hlepas NK. Is it the twilight of decentralization? Testing the limits of functional reforms in the era of austerity. International Review of Administrative Sciences. 2016;**82**:273-290

[36] Ansell C, Gash A. Collaborative governance in theory and practice. Journal of Public Administration Research and Theory. 2008;**18**:543-571

[37] Dupuy C, Defacqz S. Citizens and the legitimacy outcomes of collaborative governance: An administrative burden perspective. Public Management Review. 2022;**24**:752-772

[38] Persson E, Granberg M. Implementation through collaborative crisis management and contingency planning: The case of dam failure in Sweden. Journal of Risk Research. 2021;**24**:1335-1348

[39] Donahue J, Zeckhauser R, Breyer S. Collaborative Governance: Private Roles for Public Goals in Turbulent Times. Princeton, NJ: Princeton University Press; 2011

[40] Abou-bakr A. Managing Disasters through Public-Private Partnerships. Washington, DC: Georgetown University Press; 2013

[41] Shi Y, Jang H, Keyes L, Dicke L. Nonprofit service continuity and responses in the pandemic: Disruptions, ambiguity, innovation and challenges. Public Administration Review. 2020;**80**:874-879

[42] Steen T, Brandsen T. Coproduction during and after the COVID-19 pandemic: Will it last? Public Administration Review. 2020;**80**:851-855

[43] Larsson OL. Overcoming collective-action problems in collaborative crisis management: Meta-governance and security communications systems. In: Bynander F, Nohrstedt D, editors. Collaborative Crisis Management: Inter-Organizational Approaches to Extreme Events. New York: Routledge; 2020. pp. 57-69

[44] Boin A, Kuipers S, Overdijk W. Leadership in times of crisis: A framework for assessment. International Review of Public Administration. 2013;**18**(1):79-91

[45] Murphy P, Dunn P. Senior leadership in times of crisis. Noetic Notes. 2012;**3**:1-24

[46] Farazmand A. Learning from the Katrina crisis: A global and international perspective with implications for future crisis management. Public Administration Review. 2007;**67**:149-160

[47] Kapucu N, Ustun Y. Collaborative crisis management and leadership in the public sector. International Journal of Public Administration. 2018;**41**:548-561

[48] Cristofoli D, Douglas S, Torfing J, Trivellato B. Having it all: Can collaborative governance be both legitimate and accountable? Public Management Review. 2022;**24**:704-728

[49] Ansell C, Sørensen E, Torfing J. The COVID-19 pandemic as a game-changer for public administration and leadership? The need for robust governance

responses to turbulent problems. Public Management Review. 2021;**23**:949-960

[50] Available from: https://covid19.go.id/peta-sebaran

[51] Asmorowati S, Schubert V, Ningrum AP. Policy capacity, local autonomy, and human agency: Tensions in the intergovernmental coordination in Indonesia's social welfare response amid the COVID-19 pandemic. Journal of Asian Public Policy. 2022;**15**:213-227

[52] Setiadi, Lazuardi E. From panic to confusion to negotiation: A reflection from early response to COVID-19 in Indonesia. Humaniora. 2021;**12**:10-117

[53] Djalante R, Lassa J, Setiamarga D, Sudjatma A, Indrawan M, Haryanto B, et al. Review and analysis of current responses to COVID-19 in Indonesia: Period of January to March 2020. Progress in Disaster Science. 2020;**6**:1-9

[54] Dewi SL, Setiyaningsih H. The role of private sector in response to covid-19: A case study of DI Yogyakarta. Jurnal Kebijakan Kesehatan Indonesia (JKKI). 2020;**09**:218-224

[55] Yuda TK, Damanik J, Nurhadi. Examining emerging social policy during COVID-19 in Indonesia and the case for a community-based support system. Asia Pacific Journal of Social Work and Development. 2021;**31**(1-2):13-22

[56] Rimawan P. SONJO: An online-based social capital to minimize the adverse impacts of the COVID-19 in Yogyakarta (Kyoto Winter School 2022. Lecture 6). Kyoto: 2022

[57] Choirunnisa U, Rijanta R, Rachmawati R. Digital transformation readiness: How 'Sonjo Pangan' movement assists SMEs' product distributions during COVID-19 pandemic. IOP Conference. Series: Earth and Environmental Science. 2021;**916**:012025

[58] Available from: https://news.detik.com/berita/d-5650386/jokowi-minta-semua-pihak-kerja-sama-agar-kasus-covid-19-segera-turun

[59] Available from: https://www.unpad.ac.id/2021/02/presiden-jokowi-tekankan-pentingnya-kerja-sama-untuk-atasi-pandemi-covid-19/

[60] Thielsch MT, Röseler S, Kirsch J, Lamers C, Hertel G. Managing pandemics-demands, resources, and effective behaviors within crisis management teams. Applied Psychology. 2021;**70**:150-187

[61] Gao X, Yu J. Public governance mechanism in the prevention and control of the COVID-19: Information, decision-making and execution. Journal of Chinese Governance. 2020;**5**:178-197

[62] Bartscher AK, Seitz S, Siegloch S, Slotwinski M, Wehrhöfer N. Social capital and the spread of Covid-19: Insights from European countries. Journal of Health Economics. 2021;**80**:1-15

[63] Wu C. Social capital and COVID-19: A multidimensional and multilevel approach. Chinese Sociological Review. 2021;**53**:27-54

[64] Pitas N, Ehmer C. Social capital in the response to COVID-19. American Journal of Health Promotion. 2020;**34**:942-944

[65] Ansell C, Doberstein C, Henderson H, Siddiki S, Hart P. Understanding inclusion in collaborative governance: A mixed methods approach. Policy and Society. 2020;**39**:1-22

[66] Hanani R, Rahman AZ, Kristanto Y. Social capital and resource mobilization during pandemic: Insight from Jogo Tonggo program in Central Java. Jurnal Analisa Sosiologi. 2021;**10**:313-325

[67] Mao Y. Combating COVID-19 through collaborative governance: Lessons from East Asia. Chinese Public Administration Review. 2020;**11**:132-141

Chapter 3

Impact of Non-structural Flood Control Measures on Household Welfare in Bunyala Sub-County, Kenya

Job Lagat, Hillary Bett and Rita W. Shilisia

Abstract

Floods are the most destructive water-related disasters considered to have dire consequences on the livelihoods of the affected population. Structural and non-structural measures have been implemented as mitigation strategies to help cope with these disasters. Given the magnitude of the disaster from floods in Busia county, multiple agencies have come into play with alternative mitigation strategies. The strategies which directly engage the participation of the community are non-structural, which include flood forecasting and early warning systems, land-use planning with zoning, savings and credit schemes, and rainwater harvesting. Despite the fact that non-structural measures are considered sustainable, households in Bunyala sub-county are still struggling with the negative impacts of floods. It is therefore of interest to establish the welfare gains or profits households derive from using these measures. Descriptive statistics were used to analyze the variables of interest. Propensity score matching (PSM) is used to determine the impact of non-structural measures on household welfare through STATA software. The key finding is that households that participate in non-structural measures have their consumption expenditure reduced compared to non-participants. This, then concludes that the non-structural flood control measures have a positive impact on household welfare.

Keywords: floods, non-structural measures, welfare, PSM

1. Introduction

Flood is a water-related disaster that accounts for 54% of all water-related disaster globally and 23% in Africa [1]. Flooding may be a result of torrential rainfall or manipulation of catchment areas. Activities such as deforestation and upstream land degradation may cause excess surface water run-off, hence flooding. Floods in their most immediate effects cause the destruction of property and infrastructure, loss of lives, displacement of people, and disruption of socioeconomic activities [2]. Secondary effects associated with floods include the outbreak of water and vector-borne diseases during and after floods, loss of income, disruption and setback of ongoing development programs, and disruption of normal family life [3]. Poor households suffer the most since they rely on short-term strategies that are not sustainable and cannot adapt to long-term measures [4]. In Kenya, climate variability is commonly influenced by the complex and varied topography, altitude, lake, and sea breeze. Additionally, the complex tropical climate varies significantly between regions due to regional climatic processes such as migration of inter-tropical convergence zone (ITCZ) [5].

Major flood events that have occurred in Kenya have been documented. The 1961 floods represent one of the early attempts of studies initiated to measure the extent and magnitude of the menace. Low-lying areas were extensively inundated and widespread damage to homesteads, bridges, and other facilities was experienced. Other years affected by floods were 1968, 1977/1978, 1985, and 1990. Details of these floods are however missing [6]. The 1997/1998 El-Nino floods were also one of the major events that demonstrated to Kenya the severe devastation of the floods. This flood was further associated with land degradation, increased soil erosion, and erosion of riverbanks among other damages. In April/May 2003 floods, Bunyala was also one of the hardest-hit areas. There was complete inundation of the area; data loggers, water level recorders, bridges, and river gauging structures were carried away, affecting communication and monitoring activities. Recently, flooding frequency has increased and ranges now between 2 and 5 years. Recent noteworthy events are in the years, 2007, 2011, 2015/2016, 2018, and 2020. Approximately 50,000–150,000 people are affected each year by floods in the past decade [7].

Flood disaster management is a multifaceted approach. It involves several disciplines such as public policy and planning, economics, statistics, hydrology, psychology among others. This is because of the impacts it has on the socio-economic livelihoods of people it affects directly or indirectly [8]. Most of the measures resorted to by affected communities are of a preventive or corrective nature intended to minimize damage caused by floods [9]. A comprehensive approach to disaster management should include four basic phases: preparedness, mitigation, response, and recovery. Although most countries are focused on the last two phases, the greatest potential for minimization of economic losses and reduction of disaster vulnerability, especially among low-income groups typically lies with preparedness and mitigation [10, 11].

2. Non-structural flood control measures

Measures taken to mitigate the effects of floods can be categorized into structural and non-structural measures. Structural measures include the construction of reservoirs, dykes, diversion channels, and spillways among others. The measures are meant to reduce the effects of the flood hazard by modifying the environment through construction. However, they are associated with residual risks due to the possibility of structural failures. Non-structural measures include land use planning with zoning, water harvesting, insurance schemes, flood early warning systems, and awareness campaigns [12]. These are meant to manage vulnerability hence essential to eliminate residual risks. Kundzewicz [13] reports that these measures agree better with the spirit of sustainable development in that the objectives are economically attainable, socially acceptable, and environmentally sound. Although considered complementary to structural measures, non-structural measures may also be used alone if structural measures are not considered feasible and depending on the condition of the river basin as they may be more cost-effective [14]. They also have different implementation periods: prior, during and post-flood occurrences [15].

2.1 Land use planning with zoning

Subsistence farming is the main land activity for households in the area with farms averaging 2 acres. The main food crops grown in this area include maize, sorghum, and beans. Livestock farming mainly involves the rearing of free-range indigenous chickens at a small scale ranging from 5 to 20 birds per household. Households also engage in sand harvesting as a source of livelihood (Busia [16]).

Land use planning involves regulating how land is used and zoning endangered resources in order to ensure efficient resource use and desirable environmental outcomes.

2.2 Water harvesting

Water harvesting is among the measures earmarked for support by KIWASH through WRUAs in Busia County through the construction of water intakes, storage tanks, distribution pipelines, and pumping systems. Additionally, the program was envisaged to support capacity building among stakeholders to ensure that households benefit through access to water and awareness creation on the protection of water sources [17]. Households in Busia county have embraced small-scale water harvesting, which involves redirecting, storing, capturing rainfall, runoff, and groundwater [18].

2.3 Savings and credit schemes

Owing to the risks of floods for people residing in Busia and the possibility of destruction of crops, livestock, and homesteads, there is a need for some form of insurance. This enables households to be less vulnerable to future poverty as they can smooth their consumption in the presence of shocks and bounce back after the disaster through individual claims in case of floods. Insurance policies set in Busia county is known by very few and additionally, they would not be able to afford it. Households are therefore largely engaged in savings and credit schemes as a way of insurance from floods through engagement in social groups and cooperatives [19].

2.4 Flood forecasting and early warning systems (FEWS)

Flood forecasting and early warning systems (FEWS) is a tool that cover flood levels, likely impacts of a flood, disseminating warning messages as well as reviewing the effectiveness of the system following an event. There are significant numbers of institutional initiatives currently active in the African continent. Information regarding many of these initiatives is not publicly accessible, which results in underestimation by the wider scientific community of the amount of flood forecasting activity undertaken in the continent [20]. In 2008, the Western Kenya Community-Driven Development and Flood Mitigation (WKCDD & FM) Project was initiated by the Kenyan government with support from the World Bank to address flooding problems. This project collaborated with the Kenya Meteorological Service (KMS) which took to establishing the flood early warning systems [21].

The FEWS developed was motivated by experiences from the lake Victoria basin which recommended the integrated flood management approach. It was reported that in the 2011 flood events, there were no casualties in Bunyala sub-county as communities were warned early enough. Additionally, 1 million USD is saved annually as a result of the flood mitigation policies that were implemented. However, a picture of policy influence at the household level is lacking.

This system consists of four components that complement each other in ensuring that the system is complete and effective. These components are explained as follows:

Risk knowledge: this involves the systematic assessment of risks and hazards; mapping their trends and patterns. Upon understanding these risks, weather and river gauging stations are established considering the basin's topography, geology, and soils [12]. There are three synoptic stations in the Nzoia basin: 16 automatic hydrometric systems, three rainfall stations, and three radar water level stations: Rwambwa, Semogere, and Webuye [22].

Figure 1 shows the distribution of synoptic stations in the Nzoia Basin. These resources are used for data acquisition, which helps in the flood diagnostics and forecasting center. 1EF01 is the main pour point, while 1 BC01 and 1DA02 are sub-basin discharge stations.

Monitoring and warning system: This involves establishing sensors measuring water levels at relevant sites in local waterways and linking them to the local database. This system consists of data collection, observation, rapid communication system, processing, analysis, and database management systems. This center should be operational 24 hours a day, 7 days a week, all year round and have skilled personnel in hydrology and hydrometeorology and advanced meteorological telecommunication facilities to ensure access to data [23].

Dissemination and communication: Information is then disseminated to the dissemination center from where it is distributed to the target population and

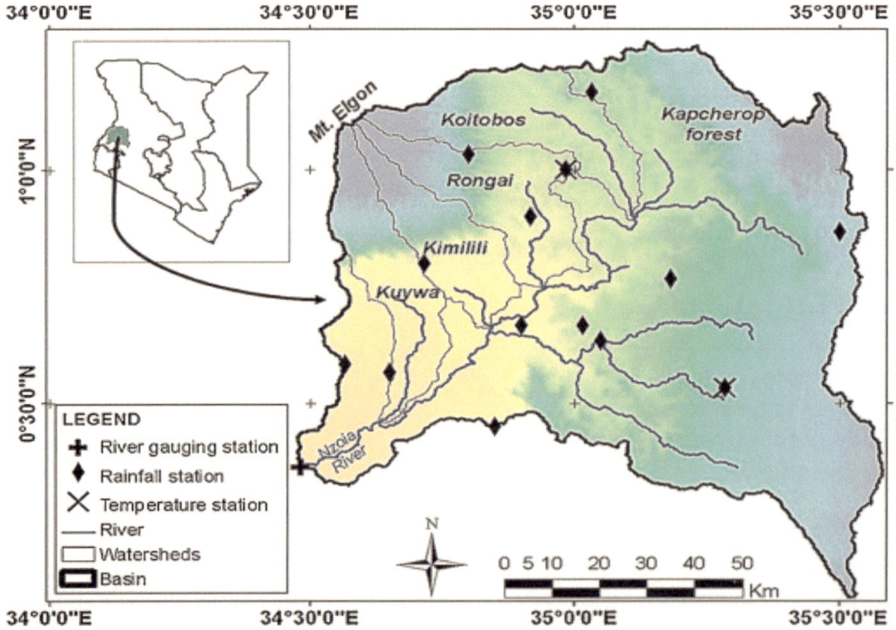

Figure 1.
Location of hydrometric and rainfall radars in the Nzoia Basin.

stakeholders. In Kenya, the flood warning and dissemination centre (FWDC) is responsible for this function. In the Nzoia basin, some users of this information include the public, Bunyala community, and emergency management like the REDCROSS, government sector, private sector, and civil societies among others. Some methods used to convey information include emails, internet websites, weather radio, and mobile short messages among others [24].

Response capability: Response plans by the communities and forecast review and development are also included in the components of EWS. It is important to have training and communication centers to create awareness and enhance preparedness. Communities are expected to also keep watch of the rainfall and water levels, provide indigenous information that can be integrated into EWS, provide flood information, provide information on impacts of floods, provide security for flood monitoring equipment and disseminate information in the local language [21].

Given the magnitude of flood disaster in Bunyala sub-county, various agencies and individuals have directly been involved in the implementation of the non-structural measures. Despite these efforts, households are still struggling with the negative flood effects. The purpose of this study is to there determine the benefits or losses households derive from these measures. The measure of welfare used in this study is household consumption expenditure.

3. Welfare and theories

The concept of household welfare explains the most commonly used proxies of household welfare, their advantages and disadvantages, and the reason behind choosing household consumption expenditure as the proxy in this study.

Theories are used to explain household preparedness and actions upon receiving warning information on impending risks. They capture cognitive skills, household needs, cultural and economic conditions that influence households' decisions to use or fail to use non-structural flood control measures.

3.1 Concept of household welfare

Welfare measures allow for the estimation of patterns in standards of living across populations over time. Consumption expenditure, asset accumulation, and income are commonly used as proxies for household welfare. Income and consumption have been debated intensely by researchers with a clear consensus on favoring consumption over income [25]. First, consumption seems to be better in capturing the concept of standard of living since individuals derive material well-being from the actual consumption of goods and services rather than from income. Consumption better reflects long-term income as it is not closely tied to short-term fluctuations; it smoothens over seasons and is less variable than income [26].

Income is more likely to be affected by seasonal patterns resulting in either an underestimation or overestimation of real income. Although collecting data on consumption is usually very time-consuming, the concept of consumption is usually clearer than the concept of income. Furthermore, it is extremely difficult to accurately measure household income, especially for self-employed households and those working in informal sectors. Finally, income is likely to be a more sensitive issue for respondents than consumption. Those who are well-off are less likely to participate in the survey or respond leading to an underestimation of income inequality among the population [27].

Assets indices are also an alternative measure of welfare. In recent years, the use of asset-based wealth indices as an alternative metric has become increasingly prominent. It has been considered superior to consumption and income as wealth better reflects long-term welfare as it is less volatile than income and consumption [28]. It is suitable for analyzing multidimensional poverty and less data-intensive hence easier to calculate. These features, however, make wealth index a specific indicator such that it cannot be comparable to conventional measures of economic status. Different studies report that the asset index is a poor proxy for current household income or expenditure even though it may reflect permanent income [29]. Some reasons limiting the use of asset bases indices are: first, this index measures household wealth relative to other households in the sample but does not quantify the households' current levels of welfare or poverty. Secondly, it has been found to have an urban bias and limited discriminatory power at the lower end of the wealth distribution. Thirdly, differences in price levels, as well as asset quality across regions, are not taken into account in the asset-based approach [29]. Wealth index, therefore, cannot be used as a perfect substitute for income or consumption, which among other considerations remain the most common and accepted measures of welfare.

3.2 Theoretical framework

A combination of theories is better in practice when explaining human behavior toward risk, especially in the natural environment [30].

The cognitive theory emphasizes the role of thinking, imagination, emotions, and values in human action. Human behavior is formed by how the person processes information perceived by the environment. According to this theory, people who receive risk information go through a sequential process that shapes their perception and behavior. Perception, in this case, refers to what people understand and believe, while the response is what people decide about alternatives in preparing and mitigating actions. This theory presumes that preparedness and mitigation behavior is a consequence of perceived risk [31].

The need theory stresses the importance that the individual places on the meaning of events and experiences. According to Maslow's theory of human behavior based on humanistic need principles, security and safety needs are important, but not more than physiological needs. The hierarchical system of needs vary between households and communities. Unless basic needs are fulfilled, safety needs such as those against natural disasters may be considered unimportant hence unobserved mitigation behavior [32].

Another theory is the cultural theory. Culture is seen as a powerful influence as it organizes a societal social structure which in turn govern people's behavior. Renn [33] has demonstrated that responses to risks are a function of cultural belief systems. A study by [30] reveals that some cultures may consider natural disasters as acts of God, inevitable and beyond human control even to mitigate the consequence; hence, very limited mitigation behavior and acceptance of recommendations of mitigation measures. On the other extreme, other cultures adopt a positive outlook, believing that technology and government action can mitigate their worst impact.

Lastly, the economic theory argues that human response to environmental risks is influenced by economic resources, hence, safety is a function of income and wealth [32]. Poorer people are more vulnerable to environmental risks because they live in houses with fewer safety measures or locations prone to various disasters [34].

Low income, therefore, prevents voluntary mitigation actions against risk. The attributes in these theories intertwine to determine the preparedness and mitigation decisions made by households. A household, for example, may be aware of the impending disaster and the mitigation measures recommended but are constrained financially or by cultural beliefs and so on as scenarios are different for individual households.

4. The study area

Bunyala sub-county is one of the seven sub-counties located in Busia County in western Kenya. The sub-county borders Samia to the north, Siaya to the east, Bondo to the south, and lake Victoria to the west (**Figure 2**).

The area experiences an average rainfall of about 750 mm and 1015 mm and has alluvial soils which support small-scale agriculture of both crops and livestock. Other activities include fishing and non-farm activities, such as petty trade. The long rains are at a peak between the months of March and May, while the short rains fall between August and October. The dry season with scattered rains falls between December and February [18].

River Nzoia drains into Lake Victoria through the Bunyala plains. Bunyala is a low-lying area with a generally flat landscape that predisposes the area to recurrent floods that occur after every 2 years on average. This can be attributed to the overflowing of River Nzoia due to the bursting of the riverbanks. This situation is aggravated by the backflow of Lake Victoria due to siltation in river Nzoia causing inundation for long

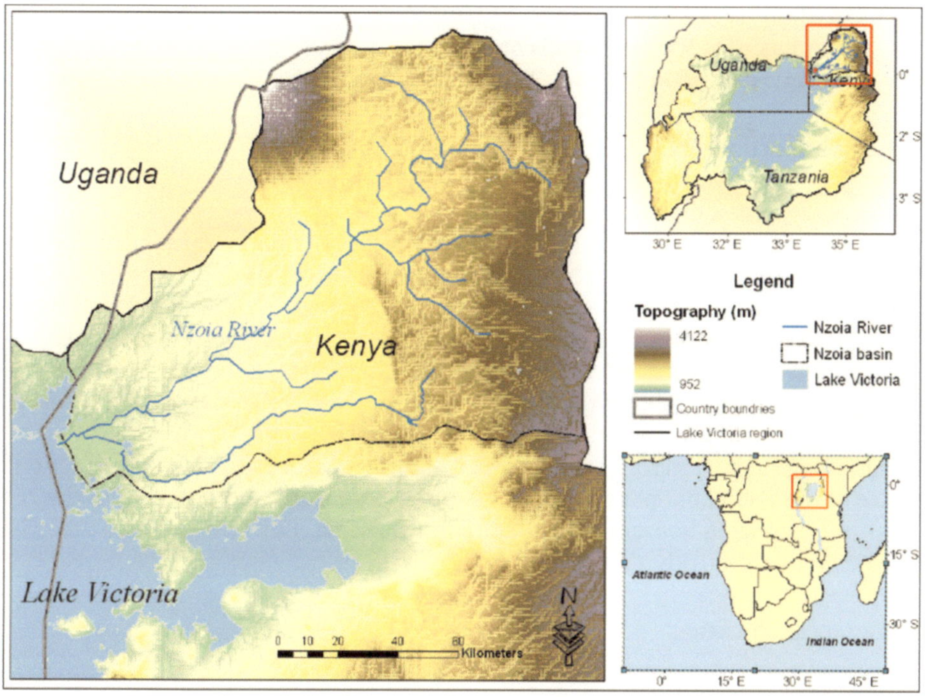

Figure 2.
Map of the study area.

periods (Busia [16]). Floods affect all the locations in the sub-county, however, those closest to river Nzoia and Lake Victoria are the hardest hit. Three sub-locations closest to the lake were therefore randomly selected for study, namely, Bukoma, Rukala, and Obaro.

5. Methodology

This section involves sample size determination and distribution among selected sub-locations. Model specification gives step-by-step procedure that will be used to determine difference in household consumption between participants and non-participants in non-structural flood control measures.

5.1 Sample size determination

The population from which the sample will be drawn consists of households in Bunyala sub-county. The sample size will be determined using Cochran [35] formula.

$$n = \frac{pqZ^2}{e^2}$$

$$n = \frac{1.96^2 \times 0.5 \times (1 - 0.5)}{0.05^2} = 384$$

where n - sample size.
p - Sample proportion (use 0.5 if p is not known).
q - 1-p.
d - Confidence coefficient (precision).
Z - Standard deviate at 95% significance level.

5.2 Sampling procedure

This study used a multistage sampling procedure. Bunyala sub-county was purposively selected as it is one of the most flood-prone areas in the country located in the lower reaches of River Nzoia.

Bukoma, Bukala and Obaro sub-locations were purposively selected due to their proximity to water bodies.

Sub-county staff, assistant chiefs and village elders were consulted to help in generating a list of households that have been in the area for at least 5 years as they have experienced at least two flood events. Respondents were drawn from the sub-location using simple random procedure. The sample size was divided in proportion to the size of the household population of the three sub-locations. According to the 2019 census, the estimated household population for Bukoma, Bukala and Obaro was 1558, 896, and 576, respectively (**Table 1**).

5.3 Model specification

Propensity score matching (PSM) was used to determine the impact of non-structural flood control measures on household welfare. In this study, households that participate in non-structural measures are used as the treated, hence participants

Sub-locations	Population	Sample Size Proportion	Participants proportion	Non-participants proportion
Bukoma	1558	197	131	66
Bukala	896	114	76	38
Obaro	576	73	49	24
Total	**3030**	**384**	**256**	**128**

Table 1.
Sample size distribution.

while those who do not are used as the control group hence non-participants. The purpose was to compare the consumption expenditure for those who took up these measures and those who did not.

Upon collecting data, there was fear that selection bias may exist, hence choosing PSM for this objective. To eliminate the selection bias, PSM uses the probability of employing the treatment propensity score (PS) to match individuals in the treatment and control group. Propensity Scores remove dimensionality issues and compress relevant information into a single value, hence making it easy to match individuals. In the estimation of the predicted values of the probability of participation, a probit model will be used as shown:

$$P(X_i) = \Pr(D = 1|X_i) \tag{1}$$

where $P(X_i)$ is the probability of participation in non-structural control measures, D = 1 for participants and D = 0 for non-participants. The regression function is as shown:

$$P_i = \varphi(\theta_0 + \theta' X_i + \varepsilon_i) \tag{2}$$

where φ is the standard normal distribution, θ' is the vector of coefficients, X_i is the vector of explanatory variables; containing confounding variables that are both related to participation and outcome and ε_i is the error term which is assumed to be normally distributed.

According to Brookhart et al. [36], one should include variables that are thought to be related to the outcome regardless of whether they are related to the exposure. This is because even if a covariate is theoretically unassociated with participation, there can be some slight chance of relation for any given realization of a data set. Including such a covariate in a PS model corrects for small amounts of chance bias, hence improving the precision of the estimator.

Baseline confounders include age, gender, education level, household size and various household characteristic. The intuition behind the inclusions of outcome variables in this study are based on the elements of the Crichton risk triangle, which capture hazard, vulnerability and exposure as the three risk components (**Table 2**) [37].

Once the model is estimated, the balancing assumption will be tested using t-tests. The sample will be stratified by PS and tested for lack of difference between the control and treatment of each stratum. After balancing, the matching process will be done.

There are different matching techniques. First, the nearest-neighbor matching which involves matching the person with the closest PS in the control group. This type

Variable	Description and Measure	Expected sign
Dependent variables		
monthlyexp	Household consumption expenditure Ksh	+
Independent variables		
hhAge	Age of household head age Years	±
gender	Gender of the household head 1 = male 2 = female	±
hhsize	Household size Number	+
landownsp	Household land ownership 1 = yes 0 = no	+
monINC	Household monthly income Ksh	+
educ	Education level of the household head 1 = primary2 = secondary3 = tertiary 4 = none	+
hhoccup	Household head occupation 1 = farmer2 = government sector3 = private sector4 = self-employed5 = unemployed6 = other(specify)	±
accesscredit	Access to credit 1 = access 0 = no access	+
EWduration	Time in days	+
floodfreq	1 = always 2 = never 3 = often 4 = sometimes	—
Savings	1 = no 2-yes	+
Consecutivefloods	1 = no 2 = yes	—

Table 2.
Covariates for propensity score matching and their measurements.

of matching can be done with or without replacement. Matching with replacement is whereby a person in the control can match more than one treated while without replacement is when once a control has been matched, it cannot be used to match another treated. Second, the caliper or radius matching involves matching individuals in the control and treatment group that lie within a bandwidth around the interested PS. Bad matches are reduced due to the bandwidth, however, if no agent is located inside the radius, then there is no match for them. Third, the stratification matching where the area around the PS overlap is partitioned into strata. Each stratum is defined over a specific range of the PS and within each stratum, there is no statistically significant differences between the treatments and control groups. Lastly, the Kernel technique where the weighted average of all observations in the control group is used to create matches for the members of the treatment group. The greater the distance between the PSs, the lower the weight. In this model, all members of the control group are used to create a counterfactual for the treatment hence, bad matches will be included. The weighting process however reduces the influence of bad matches.

Bandwidth is very important here as it determines the degree of smoothing, however, it is unclear what the correct bandwidth is hence its selection is treated as a tradeoff between bias and variance.

The nearest-neighbor method will be used to match the control and the treatment group. Each treatment is matched to the suitable control with the closest PS. However, it may be that the nearest neighbor is very far in terms of the PS. Matching with replacement will be used to address this issue hence ensuring the reduction of bias.

After matching, the average treatment effect (ATE) is estimated. The average outcome of the treatment is compared to the average outcome of the control group. The difference between the outcomes is the impact of non-structural measures on households as shown:

$$\delta_i = y_{1i} - y_{0i} \tag{3}$$

hence,

$$ATE = E(\delta_i) = E(y_1 - y_0) \tag{4}$$

where y_1 is the outcome of the participants and y_0 is the outcome of non-participants.

6. Results and findings

6.1 Region of common support

After the estimation of propensity scores, an optimal number of blocks is identified, in this case five. This is done so as to ensure the mean of propensity score is not different between the treated and control groups in each block.

When the balancing property was satisfied, the region of common support was selected. These scores lie between 0.189 and 0.996 as indicated in the table below. Observations for participants and non-participants within the region of common support were compared. Matching takes place only in the region of common support [38]. Therefore, observations showing propensity scores below 0.189 and above 0.996 were discarded.

Table 3 reports the distribution of observations in the region of common support. From 128 non-participants (control group coded 0), 57 were dropped from the analysis; these are observations whose propensity scores were below and above the minimum and maximum scores [39] while 95 were retained. For the participants (treated group coded 1), 31 observations were dropped while 225 observations were retained.

6.2 Average treatment effects on household consumption expenditure

To determine the impact of participating in non-structural flood control measures, the average monthly household consumption expenditure for participants and non-participants was compared. Matching between these two groups was attained through the nearest neighbor matching method with replacement. This is because this method is considered simple and, in case the nearest neighbor is far in terms of PS, a replacement can be found.

Inferior of block of p-scores	Participation		Total
	0	1	
0.1896932	13	3	16
.2	13	9	22
.4	18	18	36
.6	14	43	57
.8	10	25	35
.9	3	28	31
.95	0	99	99
Total	**71**	**225**	**296**

Table 3.
Participant and non-participant support distribution.

Monthly expenditure	Coef.	AI Robust Std. Err.	z	P > |z|	[95% Conf. Interval]
ATE Participation (1 vs. 0)	−3860.703	794.3921	−4.86	0.000	−5417.683 −2303.723

Table 4.
ATE effect on household expenditure.

The household expenditure was aggregated from the following expenses: food items, toiletries, housing and energy, healthcare, education, transport and communication, insurance, gifts, donations and church offerings.

Table 4 results show there is a significant difference (z > 1.96) in the household expenditures of participants and non-participants at 5% significance level. Participants are seen to have their consumption expenditure reduce by Ksh 3860.703 compared to non-participants. It can be therefore concluded that non-structural flood control measures have a positive impact on welfare.

6.3 Testing for covariate balance

There are differences that exist in observed covariates of the matched groups; hence the propensity score is used to reduce bias and balance between the treated and control group [40]. It is therefore important to access the balance of the measured covariates between the two groups. Balance means similarity in covariate distribution [41].

Covariate balance was checked after estimating the average treatment effect; to check if observations have the same distribution of estimated propensity scores. **Figure 3** reports the covariate balance using propensity scores. The factors used are as follows: household occupation, household size, education level, household age, savings, and access to credit, gender, monthly income, flood frequency, early warning duration, consecutive floods and land ownership. A perfectly balanced covariate has a standardized difference of zero and variance ratio of one [42].

The density plot for the matched sample is nearly the same, implying that matching on the estimated propensity score balanced the covariates. The conclusion is

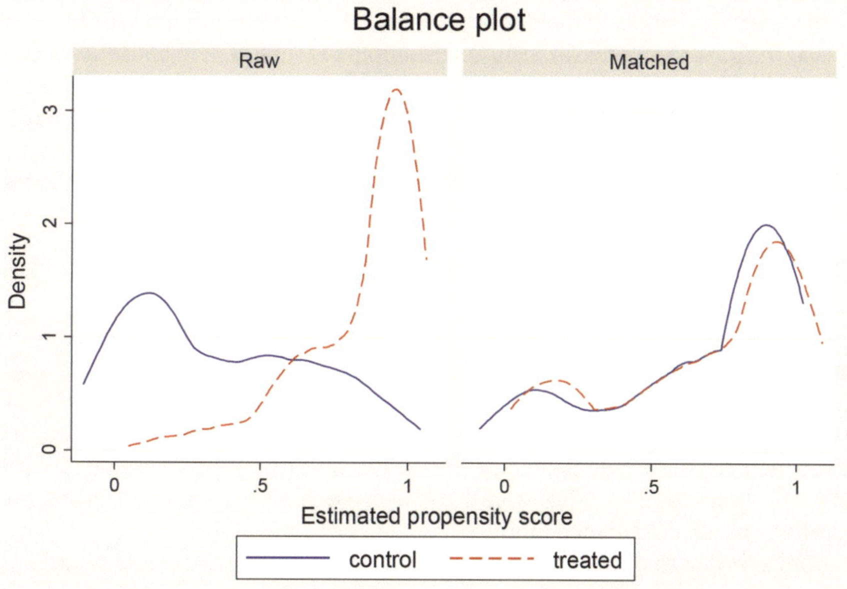

Figure 3.
Covariate balance on propensity scores.

that the covariates were well balanced and distributed in matching the participants and non-participants.

7. Conclusion and recommendations

The objective of this study was to determine the impact of non-structural flood control measures on household welfare, which was measured using consumption expenditure. Primary data were collected from 384 randomly selected respondents. Among the respondents, 256 were participants (treatment group) while 128 were non-participants (control group). To estimate the impact of these measures, household consumption expenditure was compared between the two groups, Average treatment effect (ATT) was calculated using PSM.

Results showed that the participants had their expenditure reduced by USD 38.6. Households have however reported struggles with these measures. Environmental degradation, especially land through deforestation, sand harvesting, farming along the banks, and pollution of watershed catchment areas, are features that make communities in Bunyala more vulnerable to floods [43]. I recommend that households should be given awareness and support on how to protect land and water resources so as to reduce the vulnerability of communities.

Water harvesting has also been mainly small scale and households rely on river or flooded water for consumption due to lack of resources to explore better water harvesting options. I recommend that the government in partnership with community-based organizations (CBOs) and non-profit organizations (NGO) should combine efforts in helping households install better water storage facilities.

Savings and credit schemes strategy, due to the low incomes, households tend to save less or nothing since all their income is used for consumption. I would recommend that the government with insurance companies should help households come up with a sustainable saving plan that will encourage households in the practice of saving,

For FEWS, due to unreliable information in the past, they are unable to trust this information, hence not using it. I would recommend that the KMD improve on consistency and timeliness that will relay information more accurately and hence can be trusted.

Despite all the challenges, these measures have proven essential in improving welfare.

Acknowledgements

I would like to recognize and thank my supervisors, Professor Hillary Bett and Job Lagat for their support, guidance, and contribution to this paper. I would also like to that my colleagues for their ideas and the encouragement they have accorded me, this has given me much confidence in my work.

I would also like to appreciate AERC and the support team for the research grant that has assisted a great deal in data collection. The AERC support staff for their support and encouragement.

Author details

Job Lagat, Hillary Bett and Rita W. Shilisia*
Egerton University, Njoro Campus, Kenya

*Address all correspondence to: ritawangari9151@gmail.com

References

[1] Perera D, Seidou O, Agnihotri J, Rasmy M, Smakhtin V, Coulibaly P, et al. Flood Early Warning Systems: A Review of Benefits, Challenges and Prospects. Vol. 8. Hamilton, Canada: United Nations University Institute for Water, Environment and Health (UNU-INWEH); 2019

[2] Opere A. Floods in Kenya. In: Developments in Earth Surface Processes, 1st ed. Vol. 16, Issue 1965. Amsterdam: Elsevier B.V; 2013. DOI: 10.1016/B978-0-444-59559-1.00021-9

[3] Opere A, Ogallo LA. Natural Disasters in Lake Victoria Basin (Kenya): Causes and Impacts on Environment and Livelihoods. Nairobi, Kenya: UNEP; 2006. pp. 135-148

[4] Opondo DO. Loss and Damage from Flooding in Budalangi District, Western Kenya. Loss and Damage in Vulnerable Countries Initiative, Case Study Report. Bonn: United Nations University Institute for Environment and Hunan Security; 2013

[5] Kiptum A. Seasonality, Causes, Impacts and Frequency of Floods in Kenya. Berlin, Germany: ResearchGate; 2019

[6] Programme (UNDP), U. N. D. Kenya Natural Disaster Profile; 2004

[7] World Bank. Disaster Risk Profile Kenya. Washington DC: World Bank; 2019

[8] Mohit MA, Sellu GM. Mitigation of climate change effects through non-structural flood disaster Management in Pekan Town, Malaysia. Procedia - Social and Behavioral Sciences. 2013;**85**: 564-573. DOI: 10.1016/j.sbspro.2013.08.385

[9] Neto F. Alternative approaches to flood mitigation: A case study of Bangladesh. Natural Resources Forum. 2001;**25**(4):285-297. DOI: 10.1111/j.1477-8947.2001.tb00770.x

[10] Abbas A, Amjath-Babu TS, Kächele H, Müller K. Non-structural flood risk mitigation under developing country conditions: An analysis on the determinants of willingness to pay for flood insurance in rural Pakistan. Natural Hazards. 2015;**75**(3):2119-2135. DOI: 10.1007/s11069-014-1415-x

[11] Abdul Mohit M, Mohamed Sellu G. Development of non-structural flood mitigation policies and measures for Pekan town, Malaysia. Asian Journal of Behavioural Studies. 2017;**2**(6):9. DOI: 10.21834/ajbes.v2i6.33

[12] World Meteorological Organization (WMO). Flood forecasting and early warning. Integrated Flood Management Tools Series. 2013;**19**:59

[13] Kundzewicz ZW. Non-structural flood protection and sustainability. Water International. 2002;**27**(1):3-13. DOI: 10.1080/02508060208686972

[14] Van Duivendijk J. The systematic approach to flooding problems. Irrigation and Drainage. 2006;**55** (SUPPL. 1):55-74. DOI: 10.1002/ird.253

[15] Babić M. Structural and Non-structural Measures in Flood Risk Management Case Study. Croatia: International Sava River Basin Commission (ISRBC); 11–12 November 2015

[16] County B. Integrated development plan 2018-2022. County Government of

Busia. 2018;**5**(1):86-96. DOI: 10.1016/j.ijmachtools.2009.09.004

[17] USAID. Annual Progress Report # 3 Oct 2017 – Sep 2018 Usaid Kenya Integrated Water, Sanitation and Hygiene Program (KIWASH). October. Wisconsin: USAID; 2018

[18] ATLAS. Climate Risk Profile Busia County. Nairobi, Kenya: Usaid; 1–5 April 2018. DOI: 10568/80457

[19] Otieno SA. A Comparative Study of Resilience to Flood Disasters: A Case of Kano in Kisumu County and Budalangi in Busia County. Nairobi, Kenya: University of Nairobi; 2010

[20] Thiemig V, de Roo A, Gadain H. Current status on flood forecasting and early warning in Africa. International Journal of River Basin Management. 2011;**9**(1):63-78. DOI: 10.1080/15715124.2011.555082

[21] UNISDR. UNISDR Scientific and Technical Advisory Group Case Studies – 2015 Early Warning Science: A Case of Flood Alert System. River Nzoia, Western Kenya: UNISDR; 2015. p. 2008

[22] Maina JM. Flood Early Warning System for the Nzoia River Basin. Nairobi, Kenya: KMS; 2008

[23] UNEP-DHI Partnership, UNEP-DTU, & CTCN. Early warning systems for floods. 2017. 3. Available from: https://www.ctc-n.org/resources/climate-change-adaptation-technologies-water-practitioner-s-guide-adaptation-technologies

[24] Otieno OM, Abdillahi HS, Wambui EM, Kiprono KS. FLOOD IMPACT-BASED FORECASTING FOR EARLY WARNING AND EARLY ACTION IN TANA RIVER BASIN. Vol. XLII, (September. KENYA: ISPRS; 2019. pp. 3-6

[25] Moratti M, Natali L. Measuring Household Welfare. Vol. 4. Florence, Italy: Office of Research Working Paper; 2012

[26] Deaton A, Zaidi S. Guidelines for Constructing Consumption Aggregates for Welfare Analysis. Vol. 135. Washington DC: World Bank Living Standards Measurement Study Working Paper; 2002. pp. 64-65

[27] Brewer M, O'Dea C. Measuring Living Standards with Income and Consumption: Evidence from the UK. Sweden: Working Paper: ISER, Working Paper Series; 2012. pp. 1-92

[28] Sherraden M. Stakeholding: Notes on a theory of welfare based on assets. Social Service Review. 1990;**64**(4):580-601. DOI: 10.1086/603797

[29] Filmer, D., & Pritchett, L. (1999). The The effect of household wealth on educational attainment: Evidence from 35 countries, Population and Development Review, 25, (pp. 85–120)

[30] Palm R, Hodgson ME. Natural hazards in Puerto Rico. Geographical Review. 1993;**83**(3):280. DOI: 10.2307/215730

[31] Mileti DS, O'Brien PW. Warnings during disaster: Normalizing communicated risk. Social Problems. 1992;**39**(1):40-57. DOI: 10.2307/3096912

[32] Asgary A, Willis KG. Household behaviour in response to earthquake risk: An assessment of alternative theories. Disasters. 1997;**21**(4):354-365. DOI: 10.1111/1467-7717.00067

[33] Renn O. Concepts of risk: A classification. Social Theories of Risk.

Stuttgart, Germany: University of Stuttgart; 1992. pp. 53-79. DOI: 10.18419/opus-7248

[34] Pius Mulwanda M. Active participants or passive observers? Urban Studies. 1992;**29**(1):89-97. DOI: 10.1080/00420989220080071

[35] Cochran William G. Sampling Techniques. 3rd ed. 1977. pp. 76-78

[36] Brookhart AM, Sebastian S, Kenneth JR, Robert JG, Jerry A, Til S. Olmesartan/amlodipine/hydrochlorothiazide in participants with hypertension and diabetes, chronic kidney disease, or chronic cardiovascular disease: A subanalysis of the multicenter, randomized, double-blind, parallel-group TRINITY study. Cardiovascular Diabetology. 2006;**11**(12):134. DOI: 10.1093/aje/kwj149

[37] Wolf S. Vulnerability and risk: Comparing assessment approaches. Natural Hazards. 2011;**61**(3): 1099-1113. DOI: 10.1007/s11069-011-9968-4

[38] Raufu M, Oyewo I, Abdurrasheed M. Scientia Agriculturae food demand forecast for food demand forecast for Nigeria (2016-2028). Scientia Agriculturae. 2016;**13**(1):10-13. DOI: 10.15192/PSCP.SA.2016

[39] Caliendo M, Kopeinig S. Some practical guidance for the implementation of propensity score matching. SSRN Electronic Journal. 2008;**22**(1):31-72. DOI: 10.2139/ssrn.721907

[40] Ralph DB. Propensity score methods for bias reduction in the comparison of a treatment to a non-randomized control group. Statistics in Medicine. 1998;**17**(3):2265-2281. DOI: 10.1063/1.450443

[41] Harder VS, Stuart EA, Anthony JC. Propensity score techniques and the assessment of measured covariate balance to test causal associations in psychological research. Psychological Methods. 2010;**15**(3):234-249. DOI: 10.1037/a0019623

[42] Peter AC. Balance diagnostics for comparing the distribution baseline covariates between treatment groups in propensity-score matched samples. Statistics in Medicine. 2009;**28**(25):3083-3107. DOI: 10.1002/sim

[43] GoK. Natioanl climate change response strategy: Executive brief. Executive Brief. 2010;**2009**:1-28 http://www.environment.go.ke/wp-content/documents/complete%5Cnnccrs%5Cnexecutive%5Cnbrief.pdf%5CnGovernment%5Cnof%5CnKenya%5Cn2010%5Cn-%5CnNatioanl%5CnClimate%5CnChange%5CnResponse%5CnStrategy.pdf

Chapter 4

Perspective Chapter: A Critical Futures Studies Perspective on Embodiment and the Crisis in Sensemaking

Marcus T. Anthony

Abstract

The crisis in sensemaking is the increasing epistemological and civilizational confusion about how to understand the online and virtual worlds of the 21st century. This crisis now affects online media and social media spaces, and in turn our institutions and governance. The purpose of this chapter is to use the broad framework of Critical Futures Studies to explore the importance of embodiment in the rapidly changing digital society, with a focus on the crisis in sensemaking – how humans make sense of themselves and the world in the current age. The timeframe of the analysis will be the proceeding decade (till 2032), during which time the development of an all-immersive web 3.0 (including the "metaverse") should be well underway. The prime argument of this chapter is that an improved sense of embodiment can help alleviate the crisis in sensemaking by establishing a more internal locus of control and enhancing somatic and intuitive awareness. This chapter will also apply the author's dichotomous model of Deep Futures/Money and Machines Futures as a simple framework to help situate the discussion. The final part of the chapter will suggest an alternative scenario regarding a possible path in the future of the web, namely the Mindful Metaverse.

Keywords: metaverse, digital society, scenarios, crisis, sensemaking, embodiment, futures studies, mindfulness

1. Introduction

During the following decade (till 2032), the development of an all-immersive web 3.0 (including the "metaverse") should be well underway.[1] It may be assumed that many of the problems that we now see in web 2.0 will continue in its expanded future and some problems may worsen. The crisis in sensemaking is certain to be one issue that will require much attention. In this chapter, the questions which represent the primary focus of the discussion are:

---

[1] The research contained within this chapter is taken from the Power and Presence project, and the upcoming book of the same name [1]. This research is entirely conducted and funded by the author.

- What are some potential and ideal futures of the body and its somatic intelligence as the crisis in sensemaking continues to develop in Web 3.0 and the metaverse?
- How can humans retain an experience of embodied presence in the metaverse, and access its wisdom as they attempt to make sense of their increasingly online lives?
- What are some alternative (less often discussed) solutions and scenarios to the crisis in sensemaking?

This chapter will begin with an introduction to the discipline of Critical Futures Studies, as well as one of its analytical methods: Inayatullah's [2] Causal Layered Analysis (CLA). CLA helps to deepen conceptions and dominant frames of the future, as well as generate alternative futures.

This will be followed by a brief outline of two contrasting ways of thinking about building human futures: Deep Futures, versus Money and Machines Futures [3, 4]. There then follows a brief discussion of several historical contexts to the problem at hand: the race for the Metaverse, human embodiment in the digital age, and the crisis in sensemaking. In the section follows that the argument expands upon the importance of embodiment, including an introduction to the concept of Integrated Intelligence [5], incorporating the extended and non-local conceptions of the human mind. Finally, a possible but preferred future scenario - the "Mindful Metaverse" – shall be posited.

1.1 Important definitions

The crisis in sensemaking is the growing epistemological and civilizational confusion about how twenty-first-century humans understand the increasingly online and virtual worlds of today. Related problems include misinformation; censorship; rising dissent; increasing distrust in media and governance; and the meaning crisis (including increasing conspiracy theory cultures and quasi-religious extremism) [6–8]. This crisis now affects multiple domains of institutional and government policy making.

The term "metaverse" is usually applied to mean an all-immersive, three-dimensional, virtual-reality web space. It can be thought of as a sub-component of web 3.0, which can be assumed will continue to feature many other components outside of virtual reality: including two-dimensional interactive experiences, and spaceless auditory experiences like conversation and music.

The Authentic Self is a wiser, more present, and grounded expression of self than is typically experienced by many people today. This kind of wisdom is represented in the writings of modern luminaries (far too many to name here). Those that have inspired this research include Mate [9], Jacobson [10], and Tolle [11]. These in turn draw from the long history of wisdom traditions found across the world's great introspective, philosophical and spiritual cultures, including Christianity, Islam, Hinduism, Daoism and indigenous cultures: what Aldous Huxley [12] called the Perennial Philosophy.

Finally, the term "embodiment" refers to the lived sense of connection to the body, its feelings, and wisdom.

1.2 Theoretical framework

It is crucial that humans ensure that future virtual environments permit healthy embodiment, or human intelligence and authenticity may be gravely damaged. More

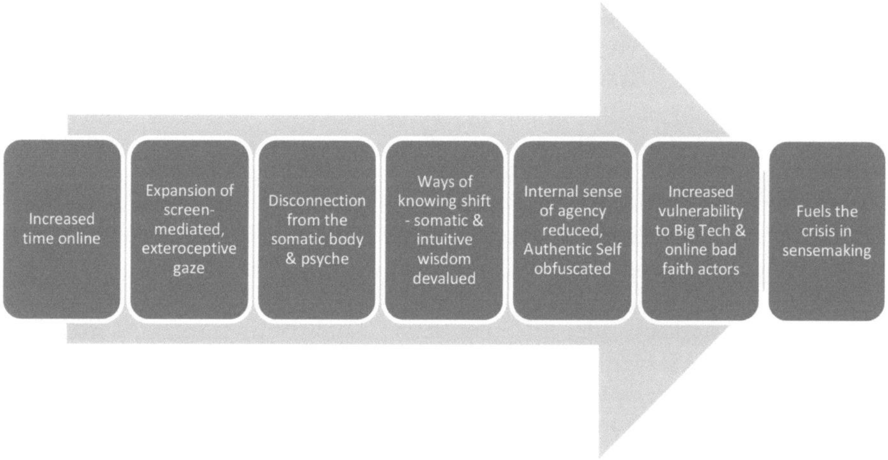

Figure 1.
How disembodiment may be fuelling the crisis in sensemaking.

specifically, this perspectival paper shall put forth the proposition that there may be a causal link between the escalation in the crisis in sensemaking and the way people experience themselves online. This can be summarised in **Figure 1**, below.

The perspective put forward in **Figure 1** is that the increased amount of time spent online and experiencing the "world" through narrow screens leads to an expansion of the exteroceptive gaze (external perceptual focus) and a consequent reduction in the interoceptive gaze (internal perceptual focus). That lessening of introspection means that people spend less time with a felt sense of the body, including its somatic wisdom [13, 14]; and less time acknowledging the psyche and intuitive knowledge [15]. There may also be a reduction in the sense of personal agency. This is because in the digital age the exteroceptive gaze is eternally outward and focused upon the often-chaotic online world, which is in turn controlled and manipulated by Big Tech and bad faith online actors; and where disinformation and misinformation are common [8]. If that causal chain holds, then interventions at any link in the chain might represent partial solutions to the crisis in sensemaking.[2]

Nonetheless, a valid query is whether an increased sense of embodiment and a change in online cultures and values can help to alleviate the crisis in sensemaking. A definitive answer will require further discussion and research, and the link that is suggested between disembodiment, the exteroceptive gaze, and an impoverished sense of internal agency remains suggestive at this point. The purpose of this paper is thus not to posit definitive answers, but to deepen the range of questions and the scope of the framework surrounding the crisis in sensemaking.

2. Critical future studies and causal layered analysis

Critical Future Studies emerged in the 1970s and were originally heavily influenced by critical theory and postructuralism; in particular, the work of

[2] Even if specific links in the chain are shown to be delimited or simply wrong, parts of the chain involving two or more related phenomena may still represent fruitful points of investigation – for example the possible link between increased time spent online and a reduced sense of embodiment.

Michel Foucault and Jacques Derrida [2]. This branch of Futures Studies is not merely concerned with trying to predict the future but also analysing the way people think about the future, as well as trying to change it. In recent decades, the movement's most prominent thinker has arguably been UNESCO Chair in Futures Studies, Sohail Inayatullah. Inayatullah [2] has outlined six pillars of the discipline.

1. *Mapping the future.* Examining the past and its lineage to the present, and how that impacts our conceptions about the future.

2. *Anticipating the future.* Identification of weak and strong trends and making predictions based on them.

3. *Timing.* This involves specifying the timeframe that one is working within.

4. *Deepening.* This involves challenging our assumptions and biases, including identifying how our worldviews and paradigms may be delimiting our thinking and visions. Causal Layered Analysis is particularly useful here, as shall be outlined below.

5. *Creating Alternatives.* Again, this includes challenging our assumptions about how humans believe the future will unfold, and positing novel alternatives. Scenario work [16] is often employed to this end.

6. *Transforming the future.* This is the realm of strategy and policy. Once stakeholders have decided upon their preferred future – which may entail the avoidance of undesirable futures – they can then set about mapping the way forward.

In the chapter to follow, the argument touches mostly upon the fourth pillar, deepening; while there is some anticipation (2) and the suggestion of a Mindful Metaverse can be seen as creating an ideal alternative (5).

2.1 Causal layered analysis

Because the process of "deepening" underpins the argument found in this chapter, a specific Critical Futures Studies method shall be referenced: Sohail Inayatullah's [2] Causal Layered Analysis (CLA). Inayatullah describes CLA as "poststructuralism as method." CLA, as shown in **Figure 2**, below, helps to deepen the view of the past, present and future by unpacking the discourse via the identification of four layers of analysis.

The four levels of Causal Layered Analysis consist of the following elements.

The litany. Here stakeholders identify the surface level of the problem at hand. This is the realm of delimited description, the reduction of problems to simplified representations. This may be deliberate, driven by overt agendas of individuals and institutions. Or it may be unconscious, driven by bias, prejudice, and projection. Typically, it is a combination of both. Any suggested or applied intervention in the crisis in sensemaking (including those in the three levels below) can be said to also be at the litany level if there is inadequate analysis, and if the identified 'cause' is not contextualised amongst other drivers.

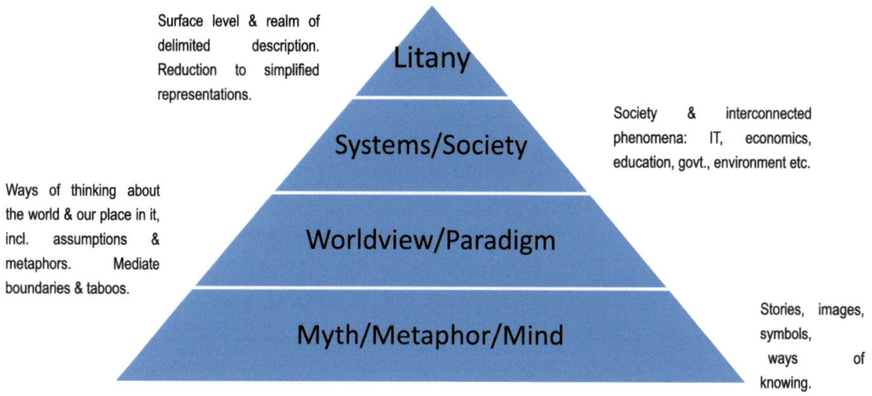

Figure 2.
Causal layered analysis.

Society and systems. More sophisticated analysis and discourse details the role of society and its multiple systems which help create the expression of the problematique under examination. These can include a myriad of interconnected phenomena, including technology, economics, education, governance, biological and environmental systems and so on. Interventions in the crisis in sensemaking at this level might employ systems-based approaches such as the legal (e.g., regulation of Big Tech and/or internet posters); technology (e.g., mandating open-source algorithms); education (e.g., teaching for digital literacy); biology (e.g., genetic modification of humans or neural chips to neutralise tendencies towards emotional projection). There are numerous other possible systems solutions.

Worldviews and paradigms. A worldview is a particular way of thinking about the world and our place in it. Paradigms are similar in that they are a set of assumptions and/or metaphors that mediate the boundaries and institute the taboos that structure specific disciplines. In Kuhn's [17] influential rendering of the idea of the paradigm, the concept referred to scientific discourses only, but it is now popularly applied more widely, including to the social sciences and humanities. "Worldview" can be applied to individuals as well as groups (industries and professions, institutions, tribes, ethnicities, religions and ideologies, countries, civilisations and historical eras and so on). However, while a "paradigm" may influence individuals, it operates via groups and collectives.

Both worldviews and paradigms tend to operate unconsciously and generate the unexamined "givens" of the discourse [2]. Thus, interventions in the crisis in sensemaking at this level would attempt to bring the unconscious boundaries of the thoughts, beliefs and narratives of stakeholders more clearly into awareness, and then expand beyond them where appropriate. Worldview and paradigm considerations represent a significant part of the argument below, where various common representations of the crisis in sensemaking are challenged.

Mind, myth and metaphor. Human stories, both old and more recent, are often drivers of what people think and what they imagine. When old and delimited stories drive people's visions, they represent what Inayatullah [2] calls "used futures." The images and metaphors that are employed in future thinking often betray biases and maybe self-constraining. Finally, the way thinkers frame human consciousness and intelligence can influence the ways of knowing (cognitive structures) that are employed to perceive and solve problems. Philosopher Ken Wilber [18] identifies three essential ways of knowing: the introspective/intuitive, the philosophical/analytical and the scientific/empirical. Wilber finds that each has its legitimate domain of application, as well as illegitimate. This chapter posits that the introspective and intuitive are crucial for developing the Authentic Self but are often devalued in our Big Tech and science-driven cultures.

The myths, metaphors and dominant ways of knowing that are commonly deployed in a given discourse may emerge from the human psyche (unconscious). Thus, unresolved personal and civilizational trauma may be an unconscious driver of any given discourse, as psychiatrist Stan Grof has long argued [15]. Bringing the contents of the human unconscious into awareness may thus assist in freeing us from its self-stultifying narratives and beliefs [2].[3]

Often the layers of CLA overlap. Its qualitative nature means that there will often be disagreements about where any given component of the analysis lies. Yet it is important to keep in mind that the purpose of using this framework is not to generate a faultless map of the focus problem but to lay out its components in such a way that the issues can be examined more deeply and at greater distance. The aim is thus to establish broader context and to bring to light the unexamined presuppositions, unconscious drivers and paradigmatic boundaries that typically remain implicit (unspoken) within the discourse.

CLA analyses can be conducted with the method explicitly and methodically applied (e.g., [3, 19]). However, a different approach is taken here, with the author regularly interspersing the text with points which emerge from all four layers of CLA, often without explicitly situating them within such layers. In this sense, it might be said that CLA informs the spirit of the article – or the underlying ideology, if one prefers more mundane language.

2.2 Deep futures versus money and machines futures

A simple dichotomy developed by the author for future discourse is that of Deep Futures, juxtaposed with Money and Machines Futures [3, 4]. Respectively, these are utopian and dystopian representations of future societies, and can be seen as emerging from two different worldviews: the techno-utopian, and the green-progressive. The purpose of this two-tier model is to help frame discussions of preferred and undesirable futures. The idea of the crisis in sensemaking can be viewed as emerging from the proliferation of Money and Machines Futures, and the diminishment of Deep Futures.

These two representations of the future are not meant to be static or metaphysically ordained systems, and stakeholders can discuss how they might be interpreted or reconfigured. Nor are they always mutually exclusive, as there may be overlaps in any given representation of the future. Nonetheless, these two disparate representations can be distinguished by their general guiding features and values.

The prime features of Money and Machines Futures are as follows.

- An Imbalanced focus upon technology and capitalist structures, which have shifted lived experience and values towards those in the list below [20].

[3] In Inayatullah's [2] Metaphor/Metaphor. The author has added "Mind," because his experience and research has led him to conclude that it is a vital to understanding futures and conducting foresight.

- Estrangement from nature, and an unhealthy amount of time spent indoors and in urban environments.

- Disconnection between the body and the psyche (unconscious).

- Perception and lived experience are essentially exteroceptive and heavily screen-mediated, while the interoceptive is diminished.

- There is a lack of psychological depth, mindfulness and psycho-spiritual awareness.

- The prime ways of knowing are "rational" or emotional projection, with suppression of somatic, embodied awareness, as well as intuitive and spiritual perception.

- Competition usurps cooperation.

- Relationship becomes increasingly online and impersonal.

- Culturally and ideologically materialistic.

- Power and wealth tend to accumulate amongst a few.

- The population resides in state of distracted amusement (computers, phones, VR), echoing Neil Postman's [21] *Amusing Ourselves to Death.*

- People's relationship with time is distorted and chronically measured for optimisation and efficiency. Populations constantly push towards desired futures. As such, people tend to lose touch with the present moment and their lived relationships with other people and places.

- Depression and anxiety tend to rise [3, 6, 22].

A poetic rendering of the Money and Machines Society is put forth in the mid-twentieth century poem *Howl*, by Allen Ginsberg [23], where he pens his thoughts on the rise of the modern industrial civilisation. Here Ginsberg metaphorically summons the dark spirit of the pagan god, Moloch, one who demands human sacrifice as means to power and control.

In Ginsberg's Money and Machines Society, humanity's intrinsic joy or "Heaven" has been consumed by the ravenous Moloch, along with its innate spirituality and embodied presence. People have become 'loveless', chasing 'unobtainable dollars' like dumb mules stumbling towards carrots on a stick, not seeing what lies beyond the dangling, desired thing. The poem reminds the reader of the demonic AI systems of much late twentieth-century science fiction classics like *Snowcrash*, *The Matrix* and *Terminator*. Humans have become 'Consciousness without a body', lost in a "Mind" of "pure machinery." And where the 'sphinx of cement and aluminium (has) bashed open (our) skulls' and consumed our 'brains and imagination" [23].

What Ginsberg could not have foreseen was the effect that the internet has had on twenty-first-century society. Nor did the initial creators of the World Wide Web fully anticipate its impact, including the rise of the crisis in sensemaking. As The

Consilience Project [20] argues, technologies are not neutral but shape personal and civilisational values. Technologies form interconnected operational systems. Those systems and their effects are typically not intentionally designed, but nonetheless via a cascade effect tip humans into futures that they have not carefully contemplated. Such futures feature new and often unanticipated power dynamics, privileged social and technological groups; and they normalise behaviour that may fundamentally shift human values and human societies [20]. In short, new technologies may unconsciously perpetuate particular worldviews, such as the techno-utopian and its dominant ways of knowing and being.

Deep Futures, on the other hand, can be seen as a more idealised alternative to Money and Machines Futures. They:

- Acknowledge the human need for material sustenance, and the importance of rational/empirical ways of knowing & being; while also permitting and encouraging other ways of knowing (including the introspective, mindful, intuitive and spiritual).

- Value and practice embodiment and presence; and the intuitive ways of knowing that emerge from that practice.

- Feature cooperation and competition, in balance.

- Value nature and sustainability and nurture a deep connection with the world and its environment.

- Value human relationships and understand the role of community in mental and spiritual well-being.

- Encourage and permit deep questions about human existence and humanity's place in the universe.

- Find importance in diversity, and the sharing of wealth and power [3, 22].

Below, the argument put forth shall be that the prophesised Metaverse – including the most well-known version that Meta's Mark Zuckerberg began to publically put forth in early 2021 [24, 25] – does not necessarily need to become a Money and Machines Future, despite the widespread criticism it has received. A more Mindful Metaverse steeped in the values and greater embodiment of Deep Futures may help mediate some of the effects of the crisis in sensemaking.

3. The context: the crisis in sensemaking, the metaverse and embodiment

The year 2021 saw the acceleration of the race for development and control of virtual and augmented reality spaces: and in particular, the metaverse. The most publicized competitor is Meta (formerly Facebook); but rivals now include Microsoft, Roblox and Epic Games, amongst others. In a CBS interview in August 2021, Meta CEO Mark Zuckerberg stated that he intends his platform to transition into a 'metaverse' company over the following five years [25]. Central to Meta's vision are Horizons Workrooms and Horizons Worlds, which will eventually encompass relationships, work, business, education and training, and entertainment. Meta's plan is to engineer a virtual future where physical, augmented, and virtual realities blend into an enhanced reality, and where economy and media become unified [25].

Zuckerberg's metaverse will thus be 'an embodied internet, where instead of just viewing content, you are in it'. His vision is of an all-immersive, all-inclusive, monetized 3D internet where future humans work, socialize, play and learn all on one platform. The Meta CEO believes that it will become increasingly difficult to distinguish the real world from digital world and that there will be no 'logging off' [25].

It is this last comment that was the source of great media and social media commentary, much of which was negative, including criticism of the potential problems that might arise in an all-immersive, capitalistic virtual universe. A common critical refrain focused upon the potential for humans to become trapped in a kind of Matrix scenario, unable to escape the clasp of the soul-sucking machines. Many pointed out that the term 'metaverse' is taken from a similarly dystopian fictional world, found within Neal Stephenson's 1992 novel *Snow Crash*, where a pizza delivery driver and hacker named Hiro has to navigate his way around a virtual universe, and where certain netizens are unable to escape [25]. These critics were warning of the possibility of the metaverse morphing into a Money and Machines Future.

Whatever the merits of these concerns, given the massive financial incentives involved, it is very probable that there will be continued expansion of virtual and augmented reality in the foreseeable future. It is expected that by 2028 the metaverse will be valued at more than 800 million dollars, while Facebook has already invested 10 billion dollars [26]. Therefore, it is crucial that the human species continues to actively monitor these developments such that we are able to deliberately and consciously exert control over the process, rather than let blind market forces dictate such a crucial shift in human technological and social development. For the cascading effects of interconnected developing technologies can morph cultures and societies in ways that distort core values, and in unpredictable ways [20].

More specifically, in this chapter, the focus is on what form the metaverse might take as it impacts human societies and cultures. What effect might it have on human minds, and how they are employed? In particular, how might a three-dimensional, all-immersive web impact the human sense of embodiment, and consequently somatic and intuitive ways of knowing? These issues will likely continue to deeply impact the crisis in sensemaking.

Stepping back for a moment, the race for meta-space can be viewed as occurring within a broader context. In the metamodern era, humans are effectively becoming more disembodied as more and more time is spent online [27–29], and our gaze is increasingly screen-mediated and exteroceptive. Humans are losing connection with the somatic body, which includes both relatively strong emotions as well as more subtle intuitions [13]. Our screen-mediated cognition is becoming increasingly dopamine-centric [6]. The concern being raised here is whether this disconnection from the body will deplete our emotional and intuitive wisdom.

3.1 The crisis in sensemaking

A further context to the race for meta-space is that this is happening amidst the crisis in sensemaking: namely, that it is becoming ever more difficult to make sense of the world and what it means to be human, as information, perception and reality itself become increasingly virtual and disembodied (Rebel [7]). Confusion abounds about what is real or true, and how people might determine such things. As uncertainty has increased, conspiracy theory culture has proliferated [30]. This is compounded by an increasing distrust of traditional media [31]. The term 'fake news' has now become deeply embedded in popular culture, while governments and institutions are struggling to influence and control populations. Amidst the increasing rapidity of the spread of mis/disinformation, policymakers must respond very quickly, often without the time required for intelligent analysis or careful deliberation [32].

It can also be noted that an associated 'meaning crisis' is accelerating. This transcends the internet age and can arguably be traced back through recent centuries. It is perhaps best encapsulated by the Nietzschean dictum, 'God is dead'. As traditional spiritual and religious cultures and life pathways have slowly evaporated across many populations, humans are faced with the age-old conundrum: just what is this life all about? [6]. Within this perspective, the crisis in sensemaking goes much deeper than mere considerations of the role of technology and disinformation. Thus, the increasing number of Americans (48%) now believing that governments should step up efforts to control the spread of disinformation online [33] may be suggesting a solution that is little more than a litany-level band-aid on civilizational cancer. This perspectival paper is therefore an attempt to initiate deeper thinking on the topic.

3.2 The authentic self and embodied presence

There are potentially multiple ways that the crisis in sensemaking can be addressed that go beyond the litany and social/systems levels of Causal Layered Analysis. Examining the issue via CLA, it can be seen that there are many levels at which stakeholders can potentially intervene. For example, as mentioned above, greater regulation of netizen behaviour and stricter control of the Tech Giants and their platforms is a common policy suggestion [33]. Yet such interventions function primarily at the social and systems level because stakeholders are attempting to change technology through the legal system, and ultimately shift online and real-world behaviour and cultures (which can be seen as entrenched social habits).

However, another approach is to go 'deeper', to examine the problem at the worldview/paradigm level (CLA, level 3), as well as intervening to shift our "minds" or consciousness structures via alternative ways of knowing (CLA, level 4). The focus taken here speculates upon the potential value of establishing an Authentic Self via the cultivation of Embodied Presence. This approach is not mutually exclusive from other hypothetical interventions at other levels of CLA, such as the technological, legal, educational and so on. This chapter's suggested approach could work alongside them.

The wisdom of Embodied Presence is expressed via the somatic body and "integrated intelligence" (which shall be defined in the following section). Elsewhere, the author has argued that modern cultures have already damaged the relationship between mind and body [5, 22, 34]. To further diminish that relationship in a metaverse-centred, Money and Machines Future would represent the perpetuation and deepening of a major civilisational error that underpins the crisis in sensemaking [5, 22].

As humanity approaches the dawning of web 3.0 and the metaverse, our burgeoning IT systems, cultures and dominant ways of knowing increasingly emphasise exteroception at the expense of interoception [14]. Most notably, exteroceptive stimuli are now typically mediated by invisible third parties and artificial intelligence, and where the drive for profit and power is typically obfuscated, along with the source code. The values of the system are designed for optimisation of the profit and power of Big Tech, and via maximising clickability of content [6–8, 20]. The system does not encourage the development of the interoceptive gaze required for human beings to develop the mindful wisdom which could help them establish their Authentic Selves and to lead meaningful lives.

4. Embodiment, integrated intelligence and the extended mind

Traditionally, human intelligence was assumed to function purely through the brain, or at least to operate via sensory inputs that operated in tandem with the brain. This still remains the dominant model in mainstream science [14, 35, 36]. The argument put forward by the author is that this model is no longer tenable, given that humans are entangled with multiple sources of information from sensory and (as shall be explained) 'extra-sensory' sources. To accommodate this expanded framework, the author has developed the model of 'integrated intelligence' [5, 22, 34].

Integrated intelligence is the (potentially) conscious and active employment of an expansive range of human cognitive abilities – including those that draw upon the mental, somatic, digital and intuitive – and which helps us to solve problems and live successfully. **Figure 3**, below, provides a crude representation of the model.

In the model suggested in **Figure 3**, the intellect or conscious mind can deliberately draw information from any of the layers of mind listed above it, and may equally draw information *unconsciously* from any of those layers. The somatic body is the feelings and intuitions that the body provides us from moment to moment, as it processes information from the environment and the other layers of the model. The psyche is

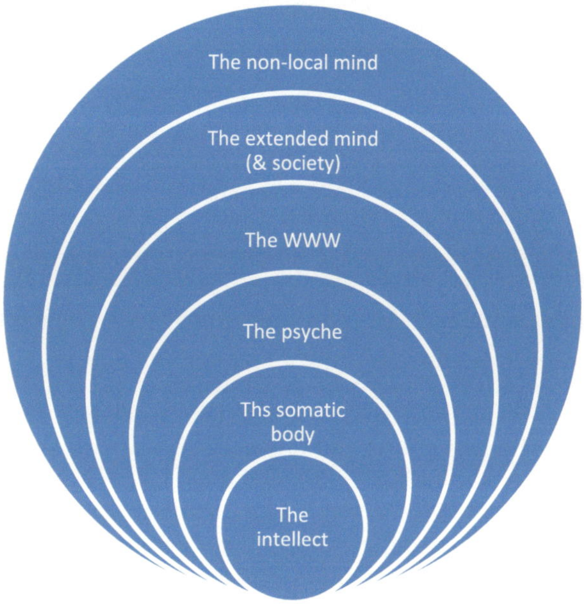

Figure 3.
Integrated intelligence.

the world of subconscious dreams, images and stories that inhabit our inner worlds. The 'WWW' is the information humans draw from the world wide web, including augmented and virtual reality systems.

The extended mind is the synchronisation effect and intuitions that emerge as human brains and bodies interact with other people and environments, which is now well-supported by experimental science [14, 37, 38].

The non-local mind, as the term is employed here, is distinct from the extended mind. The former is the field of consciousness that expands beyond the brain and the immediate environment and is entangled with other people, places and times [15, 35, 36]. The non-local mind is typically addressed explicitly or implicitly in parapsychology and many traditional cultures and spiritual traditions. It insists that consciousness has non-local properties that transcend space and time. Nonetheless, it must be conceded that the non-local mind remains controversial within mainstream science, and is an effective paradigmatic taboo [36]. Still, the author maintains that it is an extant and important part of human consciousness; and it is also crucial to the possible futures of the metaverse and human civilisation in general.

Both the concepts of the extended mind and the non-local mind suggest the importance of retaining somatic and intuitive awareness in digital futures. Yet the founding values of the metaverse and that of our civilisation's wisdom and awakening traditions appear increasingly at odds with each other. The essential argument being established in this chapter is that somatic awareness and introspection are both keys to accessing the wisdom of Authentic Self, which in turn can help address the crisis in sensemaking. They are crucial for building sustainable and preferred futures, even though they can be considered 'other' ways of knowing within science and tech environments.

But how might humanity counter the trend towards disembodied distraction, and help netizens establish a genuine capacity for embodiment and introspection, even as they continue to use the net?

5. Towards the Mindful Metaverse

Much of the discourse on the metaverse after the buzz of early 2021 has been negative and critical, focussed upon how the increasingly serious issues of web 2.0 will most likely expand in its three-dimensional version. Yet as the discussion above suggests, there are potentially more positive future expressions of the internet, including Deep Futures where integrated intelligence, embodiment and the intuitive mind flourish. There are ways that designers can create software, hardware and cultures which can accommodate an integrated intelligence. Beyond the suggestions made in the chapter above, individual netizens can develop cultural, legal, societal and economic processes which encourage the maintenance of our humanity.

This chapter has not discussed the present state of metaverse technology in any detail, as that has not been the focus. But it is undoubtedly true that humanity is in a universe far, far away from the Star Trek holodeck, or *Black Mirror*'s eternal afterlife in the episode *San* Junipero [39]. To begin with, tactile engagement and current haptics (touch, movement) are quite limited, even though hand sensors (with gestures) have recently improved [24]. Meta's Horizons platform still requires bulky Oculus VR glasses, while at least some of the software is expensive. Eye contact, so crucial to establishing rapport and the synchronisation effect [14], remains basic. There is a lack of natural pixel distribution and depth, which often causes disorientation, motion sickness and poor depth perception. Mark Zuckerberg has stated that it takes about two months for the human brain to adapt to the current Oculus hardware. Nonetheless, it is notable that he has set the goal of having netizens feel 'present' in the future of communication and work (Mark [24]).

Given that the future is by nature malleable, and that includes the future of the internet, the author's idealised scenario - the Mindful Metaverse - remains a possibility. In this Deep Future scenario [1, 3], humans will likely retain a high immersion in online worlds but create a more genuine life balance and a more embodied, humane online and offline experience. Beyond reasonable doubt, humanity's recorded information systems will remain predominantly electronic, but humans will ideally also value community, well-being and healing, along with a more interceptive psycho-spiritual development and mindfulness.

This is admittedly a utopian scenario, one which would represent a spiritual renaissance. Yet along with the balanced ideal of Deep Futures, it would also honour scientific knowledge and achievement. Thus, it would be an open society, where diversity of cognitive modalities will be permitted to flourish somatic and intuitive; philosophical and critical; and scientific-empirical. In short, in the Mindful Metaverse scenario, introspection and Embodied Presence would be balanced with reason. There would also be a healthy expression of compassion, equality, justice and cultural and ethnic diversity. Society would slow down, as cooperation would be valued as much as competition; while education systems would teach digital awareness – a practical understanding of how online systems, media and social media platforms function [40]. Thus, people's key life decision-making would be just as informed by the intuitive as by the exteroceptive (including digital information).

Though there is no space in this chapter for details, there are many direct processes which can be employed to enhance Embodied Presence and Integrated Intelligence in virtual futures, and possibly take us closer to a Mindful Metaverse where the crisis in sensemaking can be addressed at a deeper level than the merely technological or regulatory. Some of these processes can potentially be directly utilised by web, software and hardware designers, while others might best be employed by netizens in their own private, online or offline spaces. Here I list just a few possibilities.

Body awareness exercises include 'open monitoring,' and the 'soft gazing' process developed by Dor Abrahamson at the University of California, the latter inspired by tai chi [14]. The 'body scan' stress-release practice designed by Kabat-Zinn [41] is a related tool. Meanwhile breathing exercises are an old but effective mindfulness practice [1, 10, 11, 40], and they can be done while sitting at a computer, or in almost any setting. Another self-awareness tool called 'noticing the trigger point' can be combined with creative visualisation and can also help us avoid wasting precious creative energy on online drama (which could be seen as a key driver of the culture wars and the crisis in sensemaking). Physiology is what drives the anger/projection response in online environments, not merely the other's words. Physiology without immediate judgment and action soon fades, and the brain/body system returns to baseline. Eyal [42] suggests reconditioning online habits by 'reimagining' more appropriate responses to trigger points. This can involve doing regular, short visualisation sessions where a person imagines him/herself responding differently at the moments when they habitually pick up the phone, peruse emails or respond angrily to online posts. In a similar vein, people can explore the benefits of mini-rituals as means to create more desirable online habits. Experimental evidence supports the claim that short rituals can offer effective interventions to online trigger points. Eyal [42] states that rituals can help build an empowering identity, as they help people take control of personal habits. Finally, journaling can assist with developing a strong connection to the somatic body. We can keep a record of the choices we make and how we *feel* when we make them. Paul [13] details this approach in *The Extended Mind*. Such journaling can help us clarify and codify the body's emotional messages.

The tools and processes mentioned here represent just a few means by which humans can keep connected to the somatic body, as well as to intuitive intelligence in general. As Web 3.0 develops, and as the metaverse emerges, hardware and software creators, curriculum designers and netizens, in general, can keep these kinds of tools in mind and employ them (or other tools) as they create their preferred futures.

Perhaps in the next decade, something akin to the Mindful Metaverse [1] will occur in isolated pockets, just as there are netizens and groups today who use the net wisely and mindfully, balancing it with their broader lives and psycho-spiritual development. Likewise, there is no reason that the kind of Deep Future briefly described in this chapter cannot also occur in the metaverse and on Web 3.0. Individual netizens have the potential to take their power back from the system and restore their inner/outer balance.

6. Conclusion

In this chapter, it has been argued that the crisis in sensemaking – and the associated meaning crisis – have strongly intensified in the digital age, along with a loss of a sense of embodiment, presence and intuitive and somatic wisdom. The causal chain posited in **Figure 1**, above, is merely provocative and suggestive at this time, inviting the possibility of further scientific and analytical research.

Inayatullah's [2] Causal Layered Analysis was broadly applied to indicate that both causes and solutions to the crisis in sensemaking may operate at different levels. It has been suggested that deeper levels of examination which address layers three and four of CLA (worldview/paradigm, and mind/myth/metaphor) are less commonly discussed in relation to the crisis in sensemaking but may potentially be fruitful spaces to apply crisis management. The discussion of embodiment, integrated intelligence, expanded ways of knowing and the Authentic Self lie at these deeper levels.

An idealised alternative future posited by the author is the Mindful Metaverse, and it can be contrasted with the dystopian Money and Machines scenarios commonly seen depicted in popular science fiction, where the machines and Big Tech colonise the hearts and minds of our species. Several tools have been suggested that may help create what the author sees as a preferred future.

As a civilisation, humanity needs to refocus, to reclaim its sense of power as residing within, rather than as being constantly manipulated by external forces beyond its control: including the internet, bad faith influencers, Big Tech, governments, politicians and authority figures, and institutions. Despite current concerns, there is an opportunity – both within the tech industry and across broader society – to use the internet to cultivate embodied presence, return to an internal locus of control, and to re-establish a greater sense of personal empowerment. This may even go a long way towards resolving the crisis in sensemaking.

Author details

Marcus T. Anthony
Foresight and Strategy, College of Global Talents, Beijing Institute of Technology, Zhuhai, China

*Address all correspondence to: mindfutures@yahoo.com

References

[1] Anthony M. A mindful metaverse? 2022. Available from: https://mind-futures.com/4023-2/

[2] Inayatullah S. What works: Case studies in foresight. Taipei: Tamkang University Press; 2018

[3] Anthony M. Deep Futures & China's Environment. Journal of Futures Studies. 2009;**14**:19-40

[4] Anthony M. Deep Futures: Beyond Money & Machines. Risk Assessment & Horizon Scanning. Singapore: Nanyang Technological University; 2010

[5] Anthony M. Integrated Intelligence. Copenhagen: Sense Publishers; 2008

[6] Haidt J. Why the past ten years of American life have been uniquely stupid. The Atlantic. 2022;**11**(04):2022

[7] Wisdom R. The war on sensemaking. Daniel Schmachtenberger; 2019. Available from: https://www.youtube.com/watch?v=7LqaotiGWjQ&feature=youtu.be

[8] Zuboff S. The Age of Surveillance Capitalism. London: Profile Books; 2019

[9] Mate G. In the Realm of Hungry Ghosts. London: Vintage Canada; 2018

[10] Jacobson L. Journey into Now: Clear Guidance on the path of Spiritual Awakening. Perth: Conscious Living Productions; 2009

[11] Tolle E. A New Earth. London: Penguin; 2009

[12] Huxley A. The Perennial Philosophy. New York: Harper Perennial; 2012

[13] Paul AM. Interoception: How to Improve Your Gut Feeling. Big Think; 2021

[14] Paul AM. The Extended Mind. New York: Mariner Books; 2021

[15] Grof S, Grof C, Kornfield J. Holotropic breathwork. New York: Excelsior Editions; 2020

[16] Tighe S. Rethinking Strategy. Milton, Queensland: Wiley & Sons; 2019

[17] Kuhn T. The Structure of Scientific Revolutions. Chicago: University of Chicago Press; 1970

[18] Wilber K. Sex, Ecology, Spirituality. Taos: Shambhala; 2000

[19] Anthony M. Web Wide Warfare: Towards a Deeper Healing of the Online Culture Wars. The Journal of Futures Studies. 2021;**26**:33-48

[20] The Consilience Project. Technology is Not Values Neutral: Ending the Reign of Nihilistic Design. The Consilience Project; 2022. Available from: https://consilienceproject.org/technology-is-not-values-neutral

[21] Postman N. Amusing Ourselves to Death. New York: Penguin; 1981

[22] Anthony M. Embodied Presence, Covid-19 and the Transcendence of ITopian Fear. Journal of Futures Studies. 2021;**25**:25-34

[23] Ginsberg A. Howl. Selected Poems 1947-1995. Poetry Foundation. Harper Perennial; 2001

[24] Zuckerberg M. Meta, Facebook, Instagram, and the Metaverse! Lex

Fridman Podcast; 2022. Available from: https://youtu.be/5zOHSysMmH0.

[25] Zickraf R. Mark Zuckerberg's Metaverse is a Dystopian Nightmare. Jacobin magazine; 2021. Available from: https://jacobinmag.com/2021/09

[26] Bogart J. Why 2022 Is Investing In The Metaverse. Bogart Wealth; 2022. Available from: https://bogartwealth.com/investing-in-metaverse

[27] Garcia E, Di Paolo E, Jaegher H. Embodiment in online psychotherapy: A qualitative study. Psychology and Psychotherapy: Theory, Research and Practice. 2021;**95**:191-211

[28] Gomez AG. Disembodiment and cyberspace: Gendered discourses in female teenagers' personal information disclosure. Discourse and Society. 2010; **21**(2):135-160

[29] Kang S. Disembodiment in Online Social Interaction: Impact of Online Chat on Social Support and Psychosocial Well-Being. Cyber Psychology and Behaviour. 2007;**10**(3):475-477. DOI: 10.1089/cpb.2006.9929

[30] Rocha YM, de Moura GA, Desidério GA, de Oliveira CH, Lourenço FD, de Figueiredo NLD. The impact of fake news on social media and its influence on health during the COVID-19 pandemic: a systematic review. Z Gesundh Wiss. 2021;**2021**:1-10. DOI: 10.1007/s10389-021-01658-z

[31] Brenan M. American' trust in mass media edges down to 41%. Gallup; 2019. Available from: www.gallup.news.gallup.com

[32] Schwab K. The Fourth Industrial Revolution. New York: Crown Business; 2016

[33] Mitchell A, Walker M. More Americans now say government should take steps to restrict false information online than in 2018. Pew Research Center; 2021. Available from: https://www.pewresearch.org/fact-tank/2021/08/18/more-americans-now-say-government-should-take-steps-to-restrict-false-information-online-than-in-2018

[34] Anthony M. Classical Intuition and Critical Futures. Journal of Futures Studies. 2015;**1**:131-138

[35] Radin D. Entangled minds. San Franscisco, New York: Paraview; 2006

[36] Sheldrake R. Science Set Free. New York: Depak Chopra; 2013

[37] Valencia AL, Froese T. What Binds Us? Inter-brain neural synchronization and its implications for theories of human consciousness. Neurosci Conscious. 2020;**2020**(1):niaa010

[38] Vallee-Tourangeau F, Guthrie L, Villejoubert G. Moves in the World are Faster Than Moves in the Head. In: Paper presented at the 35th Annual Conference of the Cognitive Science Society, 2013. Cognitive Science Society; 2013

[39] Junipero S. Black Mirror, season 3, episode 4. Netflix; 2016. Available from: www.netflix.com/watch

[40] Anthony M. Power and Presence. Reclaiming Your Authentic Self in a Weaponised World. Zhuhai, China: Mind Futures; 2022

[41] Kabat-Zinn J. Full Catastrophe Living: Using the Wisdom of Your Body and Mind to Face Stress, Pain, and Illness. New York: Bantam Books; 2013

[42] Eyal N. Indistractable: How to control your attention and choose your life. London: Bloomsbury; 2019

Chapter 5

Risk Perceptions Following a Substandard Vaccine Crisis in China: An Exploratory Approach to Substantiating the Tripartite Model

Qiudi Wu, Xiao Wang and Yi-Hui Christine Huang

Abstract

Understanding the risk perception is essential to explaining people's judgment and decisions during drug safety crises. In addition to affective and cognitive components, the experiential facet of risk perception captures "gut-level" reactions in heuristic-based risk judgments. However, few empirical studies have explicated the validity of the tripartite approach to analyzing risk perception or examined whether experiential risk perception is a conceptually sound construct distinct from the well-established dual-factor model. Building upon the tripartite model of risk perception, this study acknowledges the current research gap and compares three fundamental components of risk perception as well as their relative capabilities to predict individuals' behavioral intention. Results of an online survey conducted shortly after a substandard vaccine crisis in China empirically support the discriminant validity of the tripartite model, which exhibits significantly better model fit than either single-factor or dual-factor models. A pretest-posttest analysis has further identified a highly controversial gap between experiential and affective risk perceptions: instructional risk message stimuli have provoked a significant change in participants' experiential risk perception but not in the other two components. Moreover, three dimensions of risk perception reveal different patterns of association with behavioral intention. Implications for risk and crisis management are further discussed.

Keywords: behavioral intention, crisis management, drug safety, IDEA model, risk communication, risk perception, vaccine

1. Introduction

Risk perception has long been a central concept in scholarship on risk analysis, risk/crisis communication, and applied psychology. Depicted as a subjective response that influences the way people act toward potential risks, risk perception was usually measured as a construct with dual factors: cognitive risk perception and affective risk perception [1, 2]. This long-held position has recently been challenged, however, due to charges that the predominant affective vs. cognitive dichotomy is overly simplistic [3–6]. Risk perception is more complex than existing accounts have led many scholars to believe, with the consequence that unexamined dimensions of risk perception have proved an obstacle to further theoretical advancements in risk judgment and decision-making.

1.1 Risk perception: dual-process and tripartite approach

The psychometric approach to risk perception analysis is deeply rooted in the tradition of cognitive psychology and the technical orientation of risk analysis [7], particularly the subdiscipline within cognitive psychology that focuses on judgment and decision-making. Early conceptualizations thus equated risk perception with probability assessments of potential hazards and vulnerabilities based on individuals' logical, rational, and rule-based reasoning [8–10]. The emergence of dual-process theory (DPT, e.g. *heuristic/systematic*, *heuristic/analytic*, *system 1/system 2*) provided a new understanding of risk perception by recognizing affective responses to risk as a significant evaluation mechanism [11–13]. In general, the dual-process model of risk perception has outlined two categorically distinct modes of processing. Cognitive risk perception represents the analytic process, which is slow, deliberate, sequential, and consciously controlled through a high degree of cognitive effort [14, 15]. On the other hand, affective risk perception denotes the heuristic process, which is fast, intuitive, parallel, and automatic with low cognitive effort and less involvement of consciousness [16, 17]. Unlike cognitive risk perception driven by probability-based assessments, affective risk perception represents an emotional reaction or response to the threat. A growing body of risk research demonstrates that negative discrete emotions such as fear, anger [18], and psychological stress [19] are of crucial importance for risk perception. In short, people both *think* and *feel* about risks [17].

As affect specifies "a faint whisper of emotion" [15] consisting of positive and negative feelings, many prior studies accentuated individuals' emotional responses to risk [20–22]. But many of these same studies lose sight of the intuitive aspect of affect heuristics. For instance, Trumbo et al. [23] analyzed perceived levels of fear, worry, and dread to operationalize affective risk perception without capturing the "real" presentative feeling that affect heuristics seek to capture. Furthermore, risk scholars in recent years have contended that the predominant dichotomy between affective and cognitive risk perceptions is oversimplistic [3–6]. Critiques have targeted the categorical foundations of DPT. Samuels [24] argues, for example, that *crossover* occurs whenever a process incorporates both type-1 and type-2 features. When an unconscious process is rule-based, it will be difficult to categorize as either rational or affective processing [25]. Hence, DPT fails to offer a sufficient description of all forms of risk perception.

Theories of experiential risk perception have thus been proposed to capture "gut-level" reactions in heuristic-based judgments [26]. Specifically, experiential risk perception is neither rule-based probability assessments nor full-blown emotional responses. It manifests experiential information processing that is: (1) holistic; (2) constructed upon associative connections; (3) experienced preconsciously; (4) resistant to change; (5) crudely integrated and differentiated; and (6) encoded in concrete images as well as metaphors and narratives [27]. In the field of marketing, an integrated framework of advertising persuasion delineates three message processing strategies—experiential, heuristic, and systematic—and suggests that consumers allocate and mobilize different levels of cognitive resources in information processing to form and correct their judgments for external biases [28]. Neuroscience also suggests that affective and cognitive perceptions are necessary neuro-processes for the formation of experiential-level feelings [29]. Still, relatively little empirical research has tested the validity of the tripartite approach to analyzing risk perception. One notable exception is the tripartite model of risk perception (TRIRISK) proposed by Ferrer et al. [3], which has distinguished deliberative (cognitive), affective, and experiential risk perceptions related to negative health events, and all three components were found to be associated with self-protective motivations in relation to cancer, heart disease, and diabetes.

1.2 Priming the experiential-affective gap

Most existing studies categorizing risk perception have centered on comparing cognitive with affective perceptions or cognitive with experiential perceptions [15, 30]. However, the major discrepancy between two-factor (cognitive-affective) and tripartite models has been the obscure yet dynamic boundary between experiential and affective facets of risk perception [1, 15]. Despite the umbrella phrase of *risk as feelings*, under which both dimensions share a significant overlap, two key distinctions define the relationship between experiential and affective risk perceptions.

First, unlike affective risk perception which focuses more on *emotion*, experiential risk perception primarily depicts *affect*. Frijda [31] defines affect as the irreducible aspect of emotion that "gives feelings of their emotional, non-cognitive character" (p. 383). As the most fundamental feature of emotion [32], affect has often been conceptualized as either pleasant (i.e. positive feeling) or unpleasant (i.e. negative feeling). According to this argument, experiential risk perception signifies nascent or inchoate affective responses [3] showcasing the general tendency to cater to good feelings and avoid bad feelings, even in the absence of any specific emotional response. On the other hand, affective risk perception pays close attention to the valence (positive vs. negative) and associated arousal (high vs. low) of affective responses to threat, which constitute essential emotions. Emotions—consisting of action readiness, strivings, intentions, and affects [33]—function as a key source for reflection and deliberation on important values in risk perception [6]. As a result, past research typically measured affective risk perception by means of emotional word lists (e.g. "worried," "fearful," "nervous") that refer to particular valences and arousals.

Second, experiential risk perception contains past experiences intuitively drawn from memory [12, 14]. Intuition is therefore another unique element that distinguishes experiential from affective risk perception. In a nutshell, experiential risk perception contains all characteristics of intuition, whereas its affective counterpart does not. Intuition manifests a process through which individuals can make decisions without rational thoughts and cognitive inferences [34]. It operates in a fast, associative, and unconscious way, granting access to preexisting knowledge and past experiences [35]. At a certain level, intuition becomes implicit memory, which cannot be recalled consciously [36, 37]. Such concepts as gut feelings, educated hunches, and the "sixth sense" have been used in association with the construct of intuition [38], which forms a subset of experiential information processing [14].

Past research tends to blur the boundary between experiential and affective risk perceptions by either combining the two components or prioritizing one over the other as the antithesis of cognitive risk perception. More importantly, the implicit memory system is typically recalled and accessed through implicit memory tests (e.g. word fragment completion, word identification, anagram solution). Therefore, cross-sectional survey questions from previous studies are insufficient to probe into individuals' experiential risk perception. Considering the incompatibility of conducting a separate implicit memory test, we utilize a fictitious stimulus as an alternative solution for obtaining experiential risk perception from our participants.

With limited heuristics for evaluating potential risks, nonscientific publics tend to rely on messages announced by government regulators and delivered through multiple channels to monitor the risk surroundings. Organizational and institutional communicators therefore face challenges in producing and distributing instructional messages that provide protective information for the public and facilitate effective risk communication. An emerging body of research has provided insight into the optimal measurement of instructional risk communication's effectiveness in terms of its effects on risk perception and judgment [39–42]. We adopt the IDEA model of instructional risk messages, which has demonstrated applicability across risk types and cultures, in order to provide an adequate stimulus for priming the distinction between experiential and affective risk perceptions. The IDEA model was developed to capture four components of optimal instructional risk message design: *internalization* (maintaining audience attention by highlighting timeliness, proximity, and personal relevance); *distribution* (multiple distribution channels of instructional information to reach target audience); *explanation* (accurate translation, in simple language, of the background, current situation, and scientific estimation of risks); and *action* (specific guidelines for the meaningful protection of self and others). Empirical evidence has proven that risk perception can be altered via exposure to IDEA components [39, 40]. However, these studies predominantly operationalize risk perception as the cognitive component of the TRIRISK model. The extent to which the other two components would be affected by IDEA messages remains unclear and provides an opportunity for probing into the potential gap between experiential and affective risk perceptions.

1.3 Behavioral intention and risk acceptance

During crises related to drug safety, organizations, policy-makers, and regulatory bodies all seek to effectively influence the public's behavioral intention. Behavioral intention, which refers to the readiness to perform certain types of action [43], is significantly associated with health protection behaviors [22]. A meta-analysis of 58 studies revealed that cancer risk perception is a strong determinant of subsequent screening behaviors reported by patients [44].

Much research has focused on the association between risk perception and behavioral intention [45, 46]. In the past decade, irrational dimensions of risk perception have become a vital source of insight into people's behavioral intention [47, 48]. Slovic et al. [49] found that risk perception could be largely a product of the way one feels about a hazard while exclusive of any rational interpretation of messages concerning that hazard. Moral emotions such as guilt, sympathy, and a sense of responsibility greatly impact ethical considerations in decision-making [6, 50]. A possible explanation for the increasing importance of irrational risk perception may be that one needs to leverage and mobilize all available cognitive resources to initiate analytic information processing [14]. Scholars compared the relative contributions of affective and cognitive risk perceptions to the behavioral intention formation of health-related goals [22]. However, little attention has been paid to the effect of utilizing nonconscious intuitions on conscious judgment and decision-making in such stances [34]. In addition, the explanatory gap between experiential risk perception and its two counterparts (i.e. affective and cognitive risk perceptions) in terms of their relative effects on behavioral intention remains underexplored.

Prior studies mainly regarded behavioral intention as a conceptual synonym of risk acceptance. For instance, Siegrist [51, 52] gauged risk acceptance with items measuring the purchase intention of products associated with new gene technologies. Ross et al. [53] examined risk acceptance by means of participants' willingness to use recycled water. These efforts presumed that if publics have a high level of risk acceptance, they would behave as though no (or very few) threats were perceived. Nonetheless, we assert that risk acceptance is not a rough equivalent to behavioral intention; in turn, behavioral intention is not a corollary of risk acceptance. Taking a cognitive processing approach, the theory of planned behavior [54] offers a succinct conceptualization of behavioral intention that distinguishes it from risk acceptance. In health risk events, risk is mostly unfavorable and accepting risks indicates the willingness to tolerate potential negative consequences. Behavioral intention, however, captures a motivational component suggesting "how hard people are willing to try" and "how much effort they are planning to exert, in order to perform the behavior" [54]. Such motivational factors inducing efforts to carry out certain behaviors are not always present in examples of demonstrated risk acceptance. Put differently, agreeing to tolerate the risk brought by the substandard vaccine crisis examined in our study may not necessarily reflect motivation or willingness to exert efforts to consume or promote domestic vaccines.

1.4 Background and empirical investigation

To explore the tripartite model of risk perception, we conducted an online survey shortly after a substandard vaccine crisis in China. Drug safety, which draws relatively little scholarly attention from risk perception experts, has been a core concern across the globe over the past two decades. Vaccines constitute one of the most cost-effective health measures an individual can take. Yet there are clear trends reflecting increased vaccine hesitancy among publics. In July 2018, the domestic Chinese vaccine manufacturer Changsheng Bio-technology Company was revealed to have provided ineffective vaccines with falsified production and quality control records. Although no injuries or side effects were reported, the crisis sparked one of China's largest public outcries in recent years, challenging both the institutional trust of public stakeholders and the crisis management of government regulators [55]. The crisis is optimal for the study of intuitive experiential risk perception due to its tendency to invoke irrational or implicit fears of vaccines that are not based on any medical evidence.

This study addresses three underexplored but closely interrelated concerns. First, it is unclear whether experiential risk perception is a conceptually sound construct that can be distinguished from the well-established dual-factor model. In this paper, we initially inspect the discriminant validity of the tripartite model's components in the context of the Changsheng crisis and posit that the tripartite-factor model has a better model fit than either the single-factor or dual-factor models (*H1*). To further investigate the nuanced gap between experiential and affective risk perceptions, we employ the IDEA model of instructional risk messages as a solution for capturing experiential risk perception. The key issue of Changsheng crisis rested on fabricated production and quality assurance records rather than any actual harm caused by the vaccines. Professional communicators also agree that the widespread anxiety expressed during the crisis was aggravated by inaccurate and inconsistent instructional risk messages communicated to public stakeholders [56, 57]. Through a pretest-posttest analysis, we examine the extent to which experiential, affective, and cognitive risk perceptions change after exposure to IDEA instructional risk messages related to the substandard vaccine crisis (*RQ1*).

Second, understanding the practical implications of experiential risk perception is still in its infancy. Upon establishing the TRIRISK model, Ferrer et al. [3] demonstrated that deliberative, affective, and experiential risk perceptions are considered separate constructs because they vary in terms of predictability of outcome variables in risk judgment and decision-making. This line of argument pinpoints the potential benefits of effective instructional communication in promoting health-protective behaviors through an enhanced understanding of risk perception. Moreover, measures applied to gauge behavioral intention differ greatly across disciplines. Crisis communication scholars, for example, employ word of mouth (WOM) to predict whether public stakeholders intend to say good or bad things about companies after a crisis has occurred [58]. In marketing and scholarship on consumer behavior, purchase intention receives the lion's share of focus [59]. Because so few studies tend to test the latent variance engendered by different behavioral intentions in the same risk context, we investigate the differential contributions of experiential, affective, and cognitive risk perception to individuals' use intention (*RQ2a*) and WOM intention (*RQ2b*).

Finally, we treat risk acceptance and behavioral intention as two self-contained constructs occurring in sequence and examine the mediation role of risk acceptance between risk perception and behavioral intention. We do so in order to obtain a more complex yet still practical comprehension of how different types of risk perception affect health risk judgments and decision-making. Specifically, we examine the extent to which the relationship between tripartite risk perceptions and individuals' (a) use intention and (b) WOM intention are mediated by their risk acceptance (*R3a-b*).

2. Methods

2.1 Data collection

We recruited 454 participants via Baidu Cloud, an online survey panel that authenticates respondents through a real-name database covering more than 300 cities across China. The sample was limited to Chinese IP addresses and those who had a Baidu account verified through their mobile phone. Eligible participants were required to indicate informed consent and briefed on the Changsheng substandard vaccine crisis at the outset. Participants were then randomly assigned to three different conditions: (1) control group; (2) treatment group A: only-E (explanation), and (3) treatment group B: IEA (all message elements addressed in the IDEA model). Participants assigned to the control group received only the pretest, while those assigned to two treatment groups completed part of the questionnaire before and after being presented with the stimulus messages, which consisted of a statement issued by government regulators. There was no missing data, because the questionnaire was administered to require a response to each item. Each participant was debriefed on the fictional origin of the stimulus exposure and paid 8RMB (roughly equivalent to 1.24 USD) upon completing the survey. Ethical approval of the online survey was granted by the Survey and Behavioral Research Ethics Committee (SBREC) at the university to which one author was affiliated.

Of all participants, 33.5% (n = 152) were randomly assigned to the control group, 31.9% (n = 145) to the only-E group, and 34.6% (n = 157) to the IEA group. Individual differences among participants were equally distributed across the three groups because of random assignments. In specific, 51.1% (n = 232) were female and 91.2% (n = 414) aged between 18 and 40 years. 81.5% (n = 370) reported having a bachelor's degree or above. In addition, 21.4% (n = 97) reported earning a monthly household income of less than 5000RMB, 38.8% (n = 176) between 5000 and 10,000RMB, 31.1% (n = 141) between 10,001 and 20,000RMB, and 8.8% (n = 40) more than 20,000RMB. One contentious issue of public concern that arose during the substandard vaccine crisis was that Changsheng was suspected of selling ineffective DPT vaccines used to inoculate children against diphtheria, whooping cough, and tetanus. 61.0% (n = 277) of our participants reported having one or more child(ren) whose care they were responsible for.

2.2 Message stimuli

To ensure the authentic feature as well as the ecological validity of message stimuli, we conducted extensive research into the substandard vaccine crisis to facilitate a thorough understanding of the crisis event. We also consulted (1) crisis-relevant official documents obtained from local, provincial, and central governments, (2) regular announcements from the Chinese Center for Disease Control and Prevention (CDC) and the China Food and Drug Administration (CFDA), and (3) the recently passed Vaccine Administration Law to validate the publicly available information about causes and consequences of the focus event.

Different statements were designed for each treatment group based on an official statement issued by the State Administration for Market Regulation (SAMR) in China. The message developed for the E-only condition contains information focused sorely on the outbreak of the crisis. It provides accurate information about what is happening and what has been done to mitigate the problem. In addition to the material included in E-only condition (i.e. source credibility, scientific information, and lucid interpretation), the message stimuli provided for the IEA group also incorporates components addressed in the IDEA model other than *explanation*, i.e. *internalization* and *action* steps to be taken for self-protection. The internalization component was designed to maintain audience attention and aid message retention by highlighting proximity and personal relevance. We accentuated proximity by stating that Changsheng sold 653,120 doses of ineffective DPT vaccines across the country. Personal relevance was addressed by depicting the fact that China's drug regulator accused Changsheng of fabricating production and inspection records related to rabies vaccines, particularly those for infants and children. Moreover, we included specific action steps suggested by the SAMR to encourage people to take proactive and appropriate action to prepare for or respond to the risks engendered by the substandard vaccine crisis. These suggestions included (1) immediately ascertaining their vaccination records and those of close relatives, (2) identifying whether they or their relatives were inoculated with a diphtheria vaccine with batch number 201605014-01 or with any rabies vaccine produced by Changsheng, and (3) calling or going to the local hospital for a timely revaccination at no additional cost.

Graphic templates for government announcements were employed to make participants' stimulus exposure more realistic. All press releases were purposefully kept the same length to rule out any external effects caused by heuristic cues other than the substance of stimuli.

2.3 Measures

2.3.1 Experiential, affective, and cognitive risk perception

A certain risk event may affect one's risk perception not only of the parties involved, but also entire industries that may have only been indirectly responsible for accident outcomes. The substandard vaccine crisis stirred a wave of criticism of the entire health care industry as Changsheng comprises a sizable share of the vaccine market in China. In order to reflect the holistic risk context and to avoid potential one-sided evaluation, risk perception was measured by assessing participants' perceptions of "domestic vaccines" rather than vaccines produced by a specific company. Items were adapted from the TRIRISK model [3] and selected based on their applicability to the vaccination crisis we focused on in this study. Participants were asked to state their agreement (1 = *strongly disagree* to 7 = *strongly agree*) with six items concerning experiential risk perception (M = 5.47, SD = 1.18, Cronbach's α = .87), six items concerning affective risk perception (M = 5.46, SD = 1.24, Cronbach's α = .91), and five items concerning cognitive risk perception (reverse-coded; M = 4.08, SD = 1.43, Cronbach's α = .93). **Table 1** presents items for each dimension of risk perception.

2.3.2 Use intention and WOM intention

Items were adapted from prior studies on behavioral intention [58, 59]. For use intention, participants stated their level of agreement (1 = *strongly disagree* to 7 = *strongly agree*) on whether they would (1) allow relatives to inject domestic vaccines, (2) select domestic products when they were next due for vaccinations, and (3) inject domestic vaccines themselves. Responses were averaged to form a scale (M = 4.35, SD = 1.52, Cronbach's α = .91). For WOM intention, in the event that their relatives or friends turned to them for advice, participants were asked whether they would (1) encourage them to inject domestic vaccines, (2) recommend domestic vaccines to them, and (3) say positive things about domestic vaccines. These responses were measured on a seven-point scale ranging from 1 (*strongly disagree*) to 7 (*strongly agree*). Three items were averaged to form a scale (M = 3.89, SD = 1.62, Cronbach's α = .92).

2.3.3 Risk acceptance

Participants were asked to rate their level of agreement (1 = *strongly disagree* to 7 = *strongly agree*) with three statements: (1) "I have a high tolerance for the potential risks engendered by domestic vaccines"; (2) "I think domestic vaccines do more good than harm"; and (3) "I can accept the potential risks that accompany domestic vaccines." Three items were averaged to form a scale (M = 4.12, SD = 1.48, Cronbach's α = .83).

2.3.4 Control variables

Demographics including age, gender, education, and income were set as covariates to control for potential extraneous effects. Moreover, two approaches were adopted to control for participants' perceived susceptibility to illness, which was found to be positively associated with the intention to vaccinate [60]. First, participants were asked whether they had one or more child(ren) and were responsible for their care (1 = *Yes*, 0 = *No*). Second, participants stated their level of agreement (1 = *strongly*

	Pretest (n = 454)	Posttest (n = 302)
Experiential		
1. I am concerned about being affected by domestic vaccines in my lifetime.	.76***	.80***
2. It is easy for me to imagine myself (and my relatives) being affected by domestic vaccines.	.79***	.83***
3. I (and my relatives) feel very vulnerable to domestic vaccines.	.80***	.80***
4. I am not confident that I can avoid being affected by domestic vaccines.	.64***	.72***
5. I would be lying if I said "there is no chance of me (and my relatives) being affected by domestic vaccines."	.67***	.68***
6. My first reaction when I hear of someone being affected by domestic vaccines is that "that could happen to me (and my relatives)."	.64***	.72***
Affective		
1. I am worried about the consequences that arise from getting a domestic vaccine.	.81***	.79***
2. I am fearful about the consequences that arise from getting a domestic vaccine.	.82***	.84***
3. I am annoyed about the consequences that arise from getting a domestic vaccine.	.77***	.83***
4. I feel angry with the consequences that arise from getting a domestic vaccine.	.76***	.85***
5. I feel discontented with the consequences that arise from getting a domestic vaccine.	.76***	.84***
6. I feel nervous about the consequences that arise from getting a domestic vaccine.	.78***	.76***
Cognitive		
1. The likelihood that I (and my relatives) will be affected by domestic vaccines at some point in the future is very low.	.86***	.90***
2. The way I (and my relatives) look after my (our) health means that my (our) odds of being affected by domestic vaccines are very low.	.89***	.92***
3. When I think carefully about my lifestyle, it seems that the probability I (and my relatives) could be affected by domestic vaccines is very low.	.90***	.90***
4. If I look at myself from a professional perspective, I realize that the likelihood that I (and my relatives) put me (us) at risk of being affected by domestic vaccines is very low.	.84***	.83***
5. Compared to the average person, the chance that I (and my relatives) will be affected by domestic vaccines in the future is very low.	.77***	.77***

Note. All items were measured on a seven-point scale (1 = strongly disagree to 7 = strongly agree). ***$p < .001$.

Table 1.
Scale items for pretest and posttest risk perceptions and standardized factor loadings.

disagree to 7 = *strongly agree*) with two statements to assess their perceived relevance: "the substandard vaccine incident has something to do with me" and "the substandard vaccine incident may affect my life." Both items were averaged to form a scale (M = 4.90, SD = 1.69, r = .59).

3. Results

Manipulation checks were conduced to measure participants' perceived internalization, explanation, and tendency to act based on the message stimuli. Immediately after reading through the message, participants in the two treatment groups were asked to state their level of agreement with statements that the message: (1) makes me realize potential risks the vaccine crisis has posed to me (internalization, M = 5.40, SD = 1.56); (2) makes me realize that the vaccine crisis is relevant to me (internalization, M = 5.55, SD = 1.42); (3) provides a succinct description of the vaccine crisis (explanation, M = 5.25, SD = 1.36); (4) provides an explanation of the crisis that is easy to understand (explanation, M = 5.11, SD = 1.47); (5) gives me specific action steps I should take (action, M = 5.05, SD = 1.59); and (6) makes me know the efficient action steps I should take (action, M = 4.89, SD = 1.70). Results of the independent-sample t-test revealed that the IEA group reported a higher level of perceived internalization (t (153) = 2.09, p < .05) and intention to act (t (153) = 3.89, p < .001) than the E-only group. But the two groups demonstrated no difference in perceived explanation (t (153) = 1.17, p = .244). Hence, the effectiveness of the manipulation in this study is satisfactory.

By conducting a series of confirmatory factor analyses, we examined a single-factor model, three dual-factor models, and a tripartite model independently based on participants' risk perception in the pretest. Specifically, we tested the tripartite structure against a one-factor structure and three dual-factor structures where: (1) affective and experiential risk perceptions were combined into a single factor (A-E); (2) cognitive and experiential risk perceptions were combined into a single factor (C-E); and (3) affective and cognitive risk perceptions were combined into a single factor (A-C). The internal reliability of three constructs was consistently high (Cronbach's α = .87 to .93).

To evaluate model fit, we adopted the multiple fit criteria by Hu and Bentler [61], which suggests cutoff values of .95 or higher for the comparative fit index (CFI) and the Tucker–Lewis index (TLI), and .06 for the root mean square error of approximation (RMSEA). As presented in **Table 2**, the tripartite factor structure was the only model that met all cutoff criteria: CFI = .97, TLI = .97, and RMSEA = .05. To compare the model fit of different structures, χ^2 difference between models were tested. Results showed that the tripartite model had significantly better model fit than the other four factor structures (see **Table 2**). Therefore, H1 was supported with regard to Chinese participants' risk perception of the substandard vaccine scandal. The tripartite model had significantly better model fit than both the single-factor model and dual-factor models.

A pretest-posttest analysis of two treatment groups was conducted using a paired-sample t-test to determine how three types of risk perception would be altered after introducing the IDEA instructional risk message stimuli (RQ1). **Table 3** presents the descriptive statistics and paired-sample t-test results. Participants reported significantly lower levels of experiential risk perception after exposure to either the E-only message, which merely explains the substandard vaccine incident (t = 3.62, p < .001),

Factor structure	Model fit							Model fit compared to TRIRISK model		
	χ^2	df	p	CFI	TLI	RMSEA (90% CI)	CMIN/ df	χ^2	df	p
One-factor	1024.0	119	<.001	.824	.786	.134 (.127, .142)	9.143	768.5	3	<.001
Dual-factor (A-E combined)	369.1	118	<.001	.951	.942	.070 (.062, .078)	3.209	113.6	2	<.001
Dual-factor (C-E combined)	910.6	118	<.001	.846	.811	.126 (.119, .134)	8.204	655.1	2	<.001
Dual-factor (A-C combined)	911.5	118	<.001	.845	.811	.126 (.119, .134)	8.212	656.0	2	<.001
Tripartite	255.5	116	<.001	.972	.967	.053 (.044, .061)	2.261	—	—	—

Note. CFI = comparative fit index. TLI = Tucker-Lewis index. RMSEA = root mean square error of approximation. CMIN/df = the minimum discrepancy divided by its degrees of freedom. Because χ^2 is sensitive to both sample size and model complexity, it is not an adequate indicator for comparing absolute model fit.

Table 2.
Model fit analysis summary of risk perceptions.

	E-only pretest (n = 145)	E-only posttest (n = 145)	IEA pretest (n = 157)	IEA posttest (n = 157)	E-only pre-post paired-sample t-test df = (1, 144)	IEA pre-post paired-sample t-test df = (1, 156)
Experiential	5.50 (1.27)	5.19 (1.28)	5.44 (1.09)	5.27 (1.18)	3.62***	2.05*
Affective	5.49 (1.29)	5.32 (1.28)	5.43 (1.18)	5.48 (1.21)	2.42*	−.58
Cognitive	4.42 (1.38)	4.42 (1.47)	3.98 (1.42)	4.08 (1.48)	.04	−1.32

Note. Standard deviation in parentheses following group mean. df = degrees of freedom. *$p < .05$, ***$p < .001$.

Table 3.
Descriptive statistics and paired-sample results for experiential, affective, and cognitive risk perceptions by message type.

or the IEA message, which further assists people in internalizing its personal relevance, potential impact, and precautionary measures ($t = 2.05, p < .05$). Moreover, participants who viewed the E-only instructional message reported significantly lower affective risk perception ($t = 2.42, p < .05$), while those who viewed all elements contained in the IDEA model did not. In contrast, neither treatment group showed significant pre-post differences in cognitive risk perception. Essentially, both E-only and IEA message stimuli prompted a significant reduction in participants' experiential perceptions, but results varied in the other two risk components.

To assess the differentiated predictability of experiential, affective, and cognitive risk perceptions for the public's behavioral intention to use and spread WOM domestic vaccines (RQ2a-b), we employed a hierarchical regression of behavioral intention on

	Use intention		WOM intention	
	B	*SE*	*B*	*SE*
Block 1: Demographics and controls				
Age	−.02	.09	−.12	.09
Gender	−.22*	.11	−.19	.12
Education	−.13	.14	−.35*	.15
Income	−.10	.06	−.10	.06
Children	.38*	.17	.43*	.18
Personal relevance	−.06	.04	−.04	.05
Block 2: Risk perceptions				
Experiential	.11	.09	−.05	.09
Affective	−.23**	.09	−.24**	.09
Cognitive	−.25***	.05	−.29***	.05
R^2	.11		.15	

Note. B = unstandardized effect size, SE = standard error. * *p < .05,* ** *p < .01,* *** *p < .001.*

Table 4.
Regressing use and WOM intentions on demographics, controls, and risk perceptions.

the three components of risk perception using pretest data. As presented in **Table 4**, demographics and controls were entered into the first block, while experiential, affective, and cognitive risk perceptions were entered into the second block. The overall model was reliable: $F(9, 444) = 6.21/8.93$, $p < .001$. Affective risk perception ($B = -.23$, $SE = .09$, $p < .01$) and cognitive risk perception ($B = -.25$, $SE = .05$, $p < .001$) significantly predicted use intention, while experiential risk perception did not. Similarly, affective risk perception ($B = -.24$, $SE = .09$, $p < .01$) and cognitive risk perception ($B = -.29$, $SE = .05$, $p < .001$) had a significantly negative impact on WOM intention, whereas experiential risk perception demonstrated no statistical significance.

In respect to RQ3a-b, we employed structural equation modeling to examine how the relationship between risk perceptions and behavioral intentions is mediated by risk acceptance. **Figure 1** presents the results of the full structural equation model with the nonsignificant paths represented by dashed lines. By and large, examination of the direct effects along each layer of the model showed that cognitive risk perception was negatively related to risk acceptance ($\beta = -.32$, $p < .001$) but positively related to both use intention ($\beta = .08$, $p < .05$) and WOM intention ($\beta = .09$, $p < .05$). Affective risk perception negatively predicted risk acceptance ($\beta = -.32$, $p < .01$) but demonstrated no significant linkage with behavioral intentions. In contrast, experiential risk perception exhibited no significant relationship with risk acceptance and behavioral intentions.

This suggests that each of the TRIRISK components influenced participants' intentions to use or orally recommend domestic vaccine in different ways. After incorporating risk acceptance as a mediator into the model, experiential risk perception consistently showed no effect on the outcome variables. However, the significantly negative relationship between affective and cognitive risk perceptions and behavioral intentions, as presented above, were partially or fully mediated by risk acceptance. In specific, risk acceptance fully mediates the relationship between affective risk

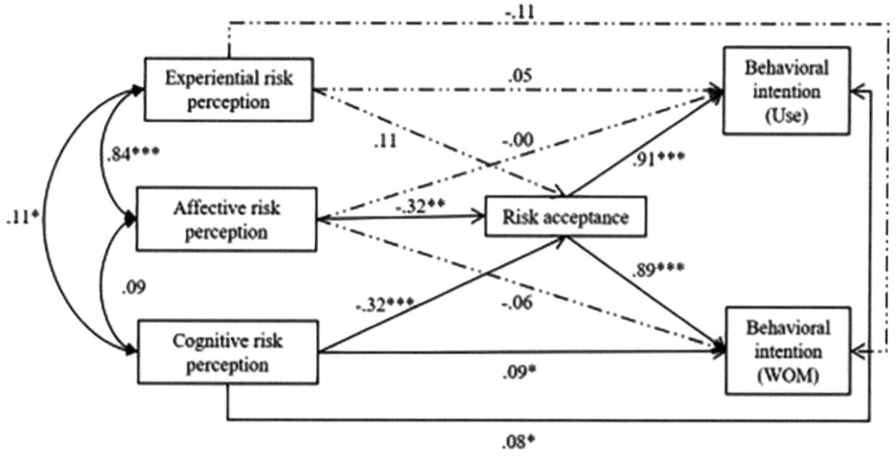

Figure 1.
Results of structural equation modeling. Note. Betas are standardized coefficients. $^{*}p < .05$, $^{**}p < .01$, $^{***}p < .001$.

perception and behavioral intentions. The fact that participants who rated higher on affective risk perception intended to reduce consumption and encourage others not to consume domestic vaccines was predominantly explained by their lower willingness to tolerate any potentially negative effects from the vaccine. Interestingly, the partial mediation role played by risk acceptance turned the significantly negative relationship between cognitive risk perception and both behavioral intentions into one that was positive. This counterintuitive finding indicates that participants who make high deliberative assessments of the risk that accompanies domestic vaccines would not be willing to tolerate the potential negative consequences but may still continue using and promoting domestic vaccines after any incident occurs. These positive associations are understandable, because participants who intend to consume and recommend domestic vaccines may feel fully informed about the scandal and generally knowledgeable about domestic vaccines, thus leading to increased expectations of coming into contact with domestic vaccines after the probability-based risk assessment. Further analyses of longitudinal data are necessary for clarifying the direction between cognitive risk perception and behavioral intentions.

4. Discussion and conclusion

Our study lends empirical support, gathered through an online survey conducted shortly after the Changsheng substandard vaccine crisis, to the proposition that risk perception consists of three fundamental dimensions that together compose the tripartite model. Past theories and models, including the health belief model [62], the protection motivation theory [63], the self-regulation model [45], and the extended parallel process model [46], mostly adopted either a unitary or a dichotomous approach to investigating risk perception. Results of our study suggest, however, that previous theoretical frameworks can be enriched and enhanced by distinguishing experiential from affective and cognitive risk perceptions. We arrived at this insight through our finding that the model fit of the tripartite model was significantly higher than that of either single-factor or dual-factor models. More scholarly attention should be paid to the tripartite model so that the conceptualization of risk perception can be explicated in greater detail.

Results of the paired-sample *t*-test demonstrated that experiential risk perception was successfully differentiated from affective risk perception. The IDEA instructional message stimuli have provoked a significant change in experiential risk perception but not in affective or cognitive risk perceptions. In other words, experiential risk perception is intuitively dynamic, whereas affective and cognitive risk perceptions are more static and resistant to extrinsic changes. According to Ferrer et al. [3], experiential risk perception is amenable to measuring via self-reports, because individuals can be aware of intuitive cues contained in survey questions. However, our study employed a pretest-posttest analysis to demonstrate that the implicit memory mobilized in experiential risk perception can hardly be retrieved through conventional self-reported responses. Instead, an adequately designed stimulus may be capable of capturing an accurate picture of experiential risk perception as well as the explicit gap between experiential and affective risk perceptions.

In contrast to previous work on the TRIRISK model, our study demonstrated that the three dimensions of risk perception exhibit different patterns of association with behavioral intentions. While this affirms once again the discriminant validity of the tripartite model, we showed that experiential risk perception is the only dimension that has no statistically significant impact on behavioral intentions. Moreover, cognitive risk perception emerges as the strongest predictor of outcome variables, whereas prior research showed that affective risk perception has the strongest predictability among the three components [3]. The case specificity and the measurement of behavioral intention might explain these new findings. Ferrer et al. [3] paid closer attention to cancer screening, on which individuals expend relatively little cognitive effort due to the low probability of negative effects on their health as a result of the screening. However, the Chinese substandard vaccine crisis involved risks that were mostly posed to children under the age of 6 years. In our study, participants were asked to measure their intention not only to use domestic vaccines on themselves but also to use such vaccines on their children and to recommend through WOM that other relatives do so as well. This is likely to arouse participants' analytic information processing and deliberative judgments. Moreover, we controlled for participants' perceived susceptibility to illness, which proves to be significantly associated with both use ($B = .38$, $SE = .17$, $p < .05$) and WOM ($B = .43$, $SE = .18$, $p < .05$) intention.

Compared with cognitive and affective risk perceptions, experiential risk perception exhibited a limited predictive power even after incorporating risk acceptance into the model as a mediator. One possible explanation for this low predictability may be participants' varying levels of familiarity regarding the risk objects. The online survey was conducted against the backdrop of a recent series of Chinese drug safety scandals, among which vaccine issues were at the center of controversies and debates. Some participants may have already formed strong opinions about domestic vaccines, while others with low levels of attention paid to current affairs may have never encountered such information. Additionally, cognitive risk perception in particular was aided by our process of providing participants with concrete information about the Changsheng crisis, which enabled them to access a rich network of cognitive associations related to the risk event. Future research could focus on unfamiliar risk objects that might lead to different findings, according to the notion that people rely more on affects and emotions in unfamiliar cases [64]. In situations of limited knowledge, individuals are more likely to access affective associations toward an unfamiliar risk object than to construct cognitive associations. Subsequent iterations of the method used here should delve deeper into the question of how unfamiliarity can make people fall back on more intuitive decision-making processes—and how that in turn affects the relationship between risk perception and behavioral intention.

4.1 Implications

Findings from this study also suggest several takeaways for risk and crisis communication practitioners and for future research. First, our results demonstrate satisfactory construct reliability and discriminant validity of the tripartite model of risk perception. This finding contributes to the two-way, audience-centric approach to defining the effectiveness of risk communication. Effective risk communication plays a significant role in both mitigating harmful actions and promoting safe behaviors. Past studies found that typical risk and crisis messages only focus on creating accurate comprehension through instructional explanation without catering to the psychological proximity of information receivers [39]. Messages with logical reasoning may only facilitate cognitive learning that elicits cognitive risk perception. Such explanation-oriented messages have a relatively limited impact on people's experiential and affective risk perceptions. In order to further enhance the reliability and effectiveness of instructional messages in risk contexts, communication professionals are expected to move beyond plain explanations and incorporate elements intended to impact irrational facets of the public risk perception.

Second, the nature of crisis events helps determine the applicability and predictability of the three components of risk perception. For instance, the risk of cancer is most often attributed to one's own habits, family history, and physique, while government regulators, companies, and other social institutions are often blamed for vaccine crises. Different attributions may provoke different ways of perceiving risk. If external organizations and institutions are the "responsible parties," the public may take more cognitive approaches to risk perception. Therefore, the nature of a specific event should be fully analyzed so that communication professionals can develop audience-centric messages that accommodate different aspects of risk perception.

Last but not least, our findings might serve as a starting point for further research on how the three risk perception components could be targeted individually and how the magnitude and direction of each component changes. Such experiments would help inform practitioners how to generate the maximum impact on behavioral outcomes. In cases of emergencies where immediate precautionary or avoidance actions are required, e.g. warnings to evacuate coastal areas because of an inbound tsunami, explanations and numeric data are useless. Visual messages, which are more capable of eliciting negative feelings and triggering past experiences with extreme weather, can be more effective in heightening experiential risk perception and may be more adequate to be disseminated in such a context.

4.2 Limitations

Our study is limited in several ways. Designed from the perspective of government regulators in the context of the Changsheng substandard vaccine crisis, this study measures only the intention to perform desirable behaviors, i.e. domestic vaccine use and WOM. Consequences and effects of these actions are restricted to participants and to their immediate family members and close friends. However, other behaviors of crucial importance to the risk and crisis management of drug safety may have consequences beyond the individual level. For instance, participating in anti-vaccine activism may impact not only individuals' lives but also the functioning of the larger community. The motivational component that drives risk acceptance to behavioral intention may vary with anticipated consequences. High levels of risk acceptance may be sufficient to motivate intentions to use domestic vaccines, but insufficient to arouse intentions to sign a petition supporting domestic vaccines. It is therefore necessary to investigate whether other types of behavioral intention should be studied. One such focus should be on communicative behavioral intention, the specific mechanism of which merits more scholarly attention considering the rapid development of social media and mobile applications. Another notable limitation rests on our sampling strategy. With respect to educational background, 81.5% (n = 370) of participants reported having a bachelor's degree or higher, far exceeding the national average of 8.73% [65]. We are thus unable to generalize our findings to the wider Chinese public. Future research should test the factor structure of the tripartite model using a more generalizable sample. Further, we also note that each participant was randomly assigned to one of the two treatment groups and exposed to stimuli over the Internet. It is unclear whether our findings would have changed—and if so, how—had participants been exposed to the message stimuli in person and in naturalistic environments. Finally, our findings may be somewhat sensitive to the case we selected, i.e. the Changsheng substandard vaccine crisis. Future studies should verify the applicability of the tripartite model to other public health crises and events.

Acknowledgements

This work was supported by the General Research Fund from the Research Grants Council of the Hong Kong Special Administrative Region, China (14616617) and the annual project fund 2022 from the Zijin Media Think Tank of Jiangsu, China.

Conflict of interest

The authors declare no conflict of interest.

Author details

Qiudi Wu[1], Xiao Wang[2*] and Yi-Hui Christine Huang[3]

1 School of Journalism and Communication, The Chinese University of Hong Kong, Hong Kong, China

2 School of Journalism and Communication, Nanjing University, Nanjing, China

3 Department of Media and Communication, City University of Hong Kong, Hong Kong, China

*Address all correspondence to: xiaowang@nju.edu.cn

References

[1] Dillard AJ, Ferrer RA, Ubel PA, Fagerlin A. Risk perception measures' associations with behavior intentions, affect, and cognition following colon cancer screening messages. Health Psychology. 2012;**31**(1):106-113

[2] Weinstein ND, Kwitel A, Mccaul KD, Magnan RE, Gerrard M, Gibbons FX. Risk perceptions: Assessment and relationship to influenza vaccination. Health Psychology. 2007;**26**(2):146-151

[3] Ferrer R, Klein W, Persoskie A, Avishai-Yitshak A, Sheeran P. The tripartite model of risk perception (TRIRISK): Distinguishing deliberative, affective, and experiential components of perceived risk. Annals of Behavioral Medicine. 2016;**50**(5):653-663

[4] Lee E. The impact of crisis responsibility and risk perception on communication behavior intention in SNS. Asia Marketing Journal. 2018;**19**(4):1-14

[5] Nihlén Fahlquist J. Vaccine hesitancy and trust. Ethical aspects of risk communication. Scandinavian Journal of Public Health. 2018;**46**(2):182-188

[6] Roeser S, Pesch U. An emotional deliberation approach to risk. Science, Technology & Human Values. 2016;**41**(2):274-297

[7] Slovic P, Fischhoff B, Lichtenstein S. Why study risk perception? Risk Analysis. 1982;**2**(2):83-93

[8] Kunreuther H, Easterling D, Desvousges W, Slovic P. Public attitudes toward siting a high-level nuclear waste repository in Nevada. Risk Analysis. 1990;**10**(4):469-484

[9] Sjöberg L. Local acceptance of a high-level nuclear waste repository. Risk Analysis. 2004;**24**(3):737-749

[10] Roh S, Lee JW. Differentiated effects of risk perception dimensions on nuclear power acceptance in South Korea. Energy Policy. 2018;**122**:727-735

[11] Alhakami AS, Slovic P. A psychological study of the inverse relationship between perceived risk and perceived benefit. Risk Analysis. 1994;**14**(6):1085-1096

[12] Epstein S. Integration of the cognitive and the psychodynamic unconscious. American Psychologist. 1994;**49**(8):709-724

[13] Peters E, Slovic P. The role of affect and worldviews as orienting dispositions in the perception and acceptance of nuclear power. Journal of Applied Social Psychology. 1996;**26**(16):1427-1453

[14] Epstein S. Cognitive-Experiential Theory: An Integrative Theory of Personality. New York, NY: Oxford University Press; 2014

[15] Slovic P, Finucane ML, Peters E, MacGregor DG. Risk as analysis and risk as feelings: Some thoughts about affect, reason, risk, and rationality. Risk Analysis. 2004;**24**(2):311-322

[16] Finucane ML, Alhakami A, Slovic P, Johnson SM. The affect heuristic in judgments of risks and benefits. Journal of Behavioral Decision Making. 2000;**13**(1):1-17

[17] Slovic P, Peters E. Risk perception and affect. Current Directions in Psychological Science. 2006;**15**(6):322-325

[18] Lerner JS, Gonzalez RM, Small DA, Fischhoff B. Effects of fear and anger on perceived risks of terrorism: A national field experiment. Psychological Science. 2003;**14**(2):144-150

[19] Sobkow A, Traczyk J, Zaleskiewicz T. The affective bases of risk perception: Negative feelings and stress mediate the relationship between mental imagery and risk perception. Frontiers in Psychology. 2016;**7**:932

[20] Lee JEC, Lemyre L. A social-cognitive perspective of terrorism risk perception and individual response in Canada. Risk Analysis. 2009;**29**(9):1265-1280

[21] Renner B, Reuter T. Predicting vaccination using numerical and affective risk perceptions: The case of A/H1N1 influenza. Vaccine. 2012;**30**(49):7019-7026

[22] Richardson JG, Trafimow D, Madson L. Future health-related behavioral intention formation: The role of affect and cognition. The Journal of Social Psychology. 2012;**152**(6):775-779

[23] Trumbo CW, Peek L, Meyer MA, Marlatt HL, Gruntfest E, Mcnoldy BD, et al. A cognitive-affective scale for hurricane risk perception. Risk Analysis. 2016;**36**(12):2233-2246

[24] Samuels R. The magical number two, plus or minus: Dual process theory as a theory of cognitive kinds. In: Keith F, Jonathan E, editors. In Two Minds: Dual Processes and Beyond. Oxford, UK: Oxford University Press; 2009. pp. 129-146

[25] Sorensen D. The unity of higher cognition: The case against dual process theory [Master's thesis]. Georgia State University. 2016. Retrieved from: https://scholarworks.gsu.edu/cgi/viewcontent.cgi?article=1197&context=philosophy_theses

[26] Sinclair M, Ashkanasy NM, Chattopadhyay P. Affective antecedents of intuitive decision making. Journal of Management & Organization. 2010;**16**(3):382-398

[27] Epstein S, Pacini R, Denes-Raj V, Heier H. Individual differences in intuitive–experiential and analytical–rational thinking styles. Journal of Personality and Social Psychology. 1996;**71**(2):390-405

[28] Meyers-Levy J, Malaviya P. Consumers' processing of persuasive advertisements: An integrative framework of persuasion theories. Journal of Marketing. 1999;**63**(4_suppl.1):45-60

[29] Damasio A. Descartes' Error: Emotion, Reason, and The Human Brain. New York, NY: G.P. Putnam; 1994

[30] Portnoy DB, Ferrer RA, Bergman HE, Klein WM. Changing deliberative and affective responses to health risk: A meta-analysis. Health Psychology Review. 2014;**8**(3):296-318

[31] Frijda NH. Moods, emotion episodes, and emotions. In: Lewis M, Haviland JM, editors. Handbook of Emotions. New York, NY: Guilford Press; 1993. pp. 381-403

[32] Batson CD, Shaw LL, Oleson KC. Differentiating affect, mood, and emotion: Toward functionally based conceptual distinctions. In: Clark MS, editor. Review of Personality and Social Psychology. Thousand Oaks, CA: Sage; 1992. pp. 294-326

[33] Frijda NH. The evolutionary emergence of what we call "emotions". Cognition and Emotion. 2016;**30**(4):609-620

[34] Lufityanto G, Donkin C, Pearson J. Measuring intuition: Nonconscious emotional information boosts decision accuracy and confidence. Psychological Science. 2016;**27**(5):622-634

[35] Remmers C, Michalak J. Losing your gut feelings. Intuition in depression. Frontiers in Psychology. 2016;7:1291

[36] Graf P, Schacter DL. Implicit and explicit memory for new associations in normal and amnesic subjects. Journal of Experimental Psychology: Learning, Memory, and Cognition. 1985;**11**(3):501-518

[37] McEvoy CL, Holley PE, Nelson DL. Age effects in cued recall: Sources from implicit and explicit memory. Psychology and Aging. 1995;**10**(3):314-324

[38] Frantz R. Herbert Simon. Artificial intelligence as a framework for understanding intuition. Journal of Economic Psychology. 2003;**24**(2):265-277

[39] Sellnow DD, Lane D, Littlefield RS, Sellnow TL, Wilson B, Beauchamp K, et al. A receiver-based approach to effective instructional crisis communication. Journal of Contingencies and Crisis Management. 2015;**23**(3):149-158

[40] Sellnow DD, Lane DR, Sellnow TL, Littlefield RS. The IDEA model as a best practice for effective instructional risk and crisis communication. Communication Studies. 2017;**68**(5): 552-567

[41] Sellnow DD, Selnow TL. Risk communication: Instructional principles. In: Thompson T, editor. Encyclopedia of Health Communication. Vol. 17. Thousand Oaks, CA: Sage; 2014. pp. 1181-1184

[42] Sellnow-Richmond DD, George AM, Sellnow DD. An IDEA model analysis of instructional risk communication in the time of Ebola. Journal of International Crisis and Risk Communication Research. 2018;**1**(1):135-166

[43] Fishbein M, Ajzen I. Belief, attitude, intention, and behavior: An introduction to theory and research. Reading, MA: Addison-Wesley; 1975

[44] Atkinson T, Salz T, Touza K, Li Y, Hay J. Does colorectal cancer risk perception predict screening behavior? A systematic review and meta-analysis. Journal of Behavioral Medicine. 2015;**38**(6):837-850

[45] Leventhal H, Meyer D, Nerenz D. The common-sense representation of illness danger. In: Rachman S, editor. Contributions to Medical Psychology. Vol. II. New York, NY: Pergamon Press; 1980. pp. 7-30

[46] Witte K. Putting the fear back into fear appeals: The extended parallel process model. Communication Monographs. 1992;**59**(4):329-349

[47] Roeser S. Intuitions, emotions and gut reactions in decisions about risks: Towards a different interpretation of 'neuroethics'. Journal of Risk Research. 2010;**13**(2):175-190

[48] Roeser S, Todd C. Emotion and Value. Oxford, UK: Oxford University Press; 2014

[49] Slovic P, Finucane ML, Peters E, MacGregor DG. The affect heuristic. European Journal of Operational Research. 2007;**177**(3):1333-1352

[50] Roeser S. The role of emotions in judging the moral acceptability of risks. Safety Science. 2006;**44**(8):689-700

[51] Siegrist M. A causal model explaining the perception and acceptance of gene technology. Journal of Applied Social Psychology. 1999;**29**(10):2093-2106

[52] Siegrist M. The influence of trust and perceptions of risks and benefits on

the acceptance of gene technology. Risk Analysis. 2000;**20**(2):195-204

[53] Ross VL, Fielding KS, Louis WR. Social trust, risk perceptions and public acceptance of recycled water: Testing a social-psychological model. Journal of Environmental Management. 2014;**137**(C):61-68

[54] Ajzen I. The theory of planned behavior. Organizational Behavior and Human Decision Processes. 1991;**50**(2):179-211

[55] Kuo L. China: Outcry over sale of 250,000 faulty vaccines prompts investigation. The Guardian. 2018. Retrieved Oct 7, 2018, from: https://www.theguardian.com/world/2018/jul/23/china-outcry-over-sale-of-250000-faulty-vaccines-prompts-investigation

[56] Jourdan A. The unfolding of China's Changsheng vaccine scandal. 2018. Reuters. Retrieved Oct 25, 2018, from: https://uk.reuters.com/article/uk-china-vaccines-timeline-factbox/the-unfolding-of-chinas-changsheng-vaccine-scandal-idUKKBN1KE1M4

[57] Leng S, Huang K. As new vaccine scandal grips China, parents say they've lost faith in the system. South China Morning Post. 2018. Retrieved Oct 7, 2018, from: https://www.scmp.com/news/china/policies-politics/article/2156357/new-vaccine-scandal-grips-china-parents-say-theyve-lost

[58] Coombs WT, Holladay SJ. Comparing apology to equivalent crisis response strategies: Clarifying apology's role and value in crisis communication. Public Relations Review. 2008;**34**(3):252-257

[59] Grewal D, Monroe KB, Krishnan R. The effects of price-comparison advertising on buyers' perceptions of acquisition value, transaction value, and behavioral intentions. Journal of Marketing. 1998;**62**(2):46-59

[60] Chen N-TN. Predicting vaccination intention and benefit and risk perceptions: The incorporation of affect, trust, and television influence in a dual-mode model. Risk Analysis. 2015;**35**(7):1268-1280

[61] Hu L-T, Bentler PM. Cutoff criteria for fit indexes in covariance structure analysis: Conventional criteria versus new alternatives. Structural Equation Modeling: A Multidisciplinary Journal. 1999;**6**(1):1-55

[62] Rosenstock I. The health belief model and preventive behavior. Health Education Monographs. 1974;**2**(4):354-386

[63] Rogers RW. A protection motivation theory of fear appeals and attitude change. The Journal of Psychology. 1975;**91**(1):93-114

[64] Plessner H, Czenna S. The benefits of intuition. In: Plessner H, Betsch C, Betsch T, editors. Intuition in Judgment and Decision Making. Mahwah, NJ: Lawrence Erlbaum Associates; 2008. pp. 251-265

[65] National Bureau of Statistics. National census data 2010. 2011. Retrieved Oct 30, 2018, Available from: http://www.stats.gov.cn/tjsj/tjgb/rkpcgb/qgrkpcgb/201104/t20110428_30327.html

Chapter 6

The Challenges of Public Service Organizations in Emergency, Crisis, and Disaster Management

James P. Welch

Abstract

The Crisis and Disaster Management process (CDMP) is composed of several clearly defined phases. Strategic risk assessment; preparation and planning, effective response and recovery, and post-crisis evaluation. It is essential for those facing such threats to understand, appreciate, and implement the appropriate responses for each phase. Public service organizations, or PSOs, are increasingly charged with additional duties and responsibilities that historically were not part of their original purview. PSOs are currently forced to operate within an environment of increasing political unrest and social chaos. Events of international magnitude now impact the domestic environment. These organizations must deal with negative media, hostile public backlash, increased scrutiny, and calls for greater accountability. Service organizations are currently faced with increasing political and social chaos, with widespread civil unrest, domestic and international threats of terrorism, human trafficking and illegal migration, public health emergencies, natural disasters, and diverse climate-related challenges. These conditions have fostered additional layers of responsibility to already overburdened first responders and their civil support partners. The consequences are significant. These previously mentioned burdens are further compounded by budgetary constraints, greater regulatory compliance, and organizational accountability. In other words, agencies and departments are expected to do more with less, much more with much less.

Keywords: risk, crisis, disaster, interoperability, communications, recovery, public service organizations

1. Introduction

This chapter will apply to all public service organizations who find themselves in the midst of a crisis or disaster event. The lessons contained in this chapter are, therefore, equally applicable to other public service organizations (PSOs) such as medical, fire, social services, public utilities (electric, water, sewage, and gas), civil defense, and roadway assistance (towing and the like), which are often neglected or even entirely overlooked. This chapter will include a strong focus on law enforcement roles and responsibilities, as they are often the first organization to be tasked with immediate response[1]. Unlike other PSOs, their activity spans the entirety of and crisis and disaster event.

According to Quarantelli [2], Such a holistic approach focuses on and encompasses concepts such as careful planning and preparation, complemented by the efficient allocation of limited resources, solid leadership, enhanced problem solving and decision making (PSDM), robust interagency collaboration, effective and timely communications, and development of a well-organized operational response, followed up by a thorough post crisis evaluation and learning to improve from any errors committed along the way. All of these factors will contribute to fostering a positive image of the responding agency involved, maintaining their all-important reputation, and ensuring public trust and cooperation. In the case study of Hurricane Katrina, reputational damage as a direct result of incompetence was on full display. Individuals in positions of local and national power were fired or otherwise held accountable. President George W. Bush Jr. lost any hope of reelection following the muddled response.

One might be excused for considering the role of these stakeholders to be a well-defined and straightforward proposition during crisis and disaster events, but nothing could be further from the truth. Research has also indicated that the public lacks resilience and is often unprepared in the face of such events, due to the misperception that PSOs will take care of the situation without the need for additional assistance. The truth is that citizens, and the private sector, both have a moral responsibility and an ethical obligation to assist public service organizations in times of need. It has become increasingly apparent that crisis and disaster management is a community concern and that, in order to establish proper resilience, the public and private sectors must also play an active supporting role. Initiatives are such as private-public partnerships.

2. The crisis and disaster management process (CDMP)

As might well be imagined, there exist several phases when passing from risk status to a full-blown disaster. Risk, whether know, perceived, or unknown, is the first stage of this process. It is important to bear in mind that risk can be both perceived and experienced as either positive or negative. This is followed by threats these are dangers that are posed but as yet remain unmanifested, whereas a *hazard* is a source or situation that presents harmful consequences to persons, property, the environment, or any combination thereof. These two terms are often conflated and understandably so! This is the reason only one term was employed here. Generally speaking, hazard is a term employed when speaking of a condition, which may lead to an accident event, or alternatively non-manmade events, whereas threats are often confined to human behavior, such as a bomb threat, or the threat of violence.

Thus, a threat arises out of risks and once a threat actually manifests itself, it can result in a number of different conditions ranging in seriousness. The gravity of such incidents helps to clarify and categorize them. Such incidents may range in severity from a minor incident to an accident and from an emergency situation up to and including a crisis or disaster event. A disaster that grows beyond the control of the responding organization may eventually rise to the level of a catastrophe or calamity. In such situations, the future remains unclear, with no conceivable solution, and there is a corresponding total loss of control by responding agents (**Figure 1**).

2.1 Defining emergencies, critical events, crises, and disasters

Let us begin by clearly defining the difference between a crisis and a disaster. Steven Fink ([3], p. 7) defines a crisis, as "*...a fluid and dynamic state of affairs*

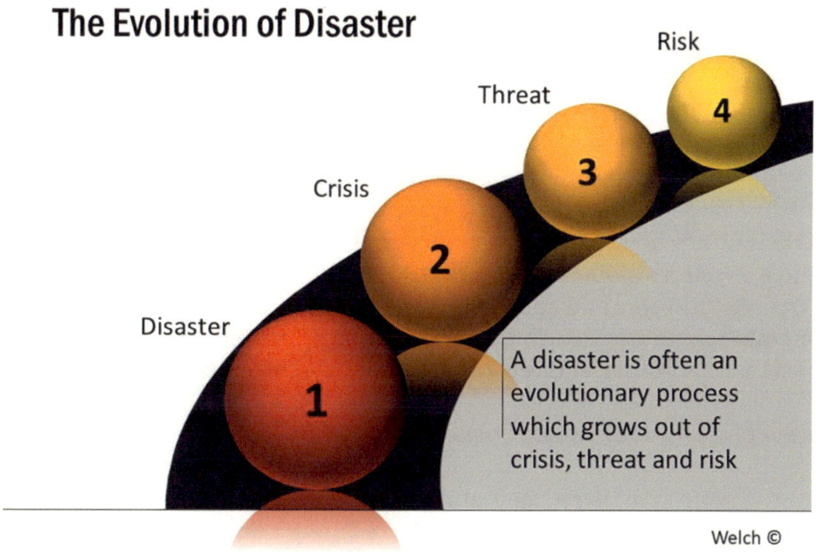

Figure 1.
The evolutionary development from risk to disaster.

containing equal parts danger and opportunity." The author then goes on to clarify that, "*It is a turning point for better or worse.*" He relates this to the Chinese term for crisis 危機 (pronounced wei-ji in English). Victor H. Mair tends to disagree pedantically stating "Like most Mandarin words, that for 'crisis' (weijı) consists of two syllables that are written with two separate characters, wēi (危) and jī (機/机)."[1] Whatever the case may be regarding semantic accuracy, the interpretation as presented by Fink has taken root in the world of CDMP. Bear in mind however that many dispute this interpretation.

Importantly, while this chiaroscuro perspective, when considered in the context of risk, posits that there exist both opportunities and threats. This relates directly to what we refer to as risk appetite. In other words, how much risk are we willing to accept or tolerate in exchange for a perceived benefit? We can also apply this perception to our understanding of a crisis since a crisis is inevitably the result of a risk.

Interestingly, Otto Lerbinger (Chapter 3; p. 45), for his part, sees risk as closely related to the media coverage an emergency event generates and remarks that there exist extremes in perception of what actually constitutes a crisis. The researchers Boin et al. [4]: 163) draw a connection between crises and disasters by elucidating that a "crisis... pertains to the process of perceived disruption; "whereas "disaster applies to the collectively arrived-at appraisal of such a process in negative terms. In this perspective, a disaster is a crisis with a bad ending." In other words, there is no clear-cut definition that delineates these two phenomena, and they remain largely subjective in nature.

It is useful to also understand the semantic and conceptual difference between what constitutes a critical event and that of a crisis. A critical incident may be considered as an *ambiguous and often threatening situation* where a routine, emergency situation has the capacity to evolve into a crisis. A crisis surpasses the capabilities, available resources or training of the responding agency and results in an ambiguous or uncertain outcome.

[1] There has been some pedantic controversy related to defining "jī (機/机)" as opportunity. For further clarification on this topic the reader is referred to: http://www.pinyin.info/chinese/crisis.html.

While crises take on a variety of forms and are composed of distinct characteristics, here we are primarily concerned with intrinsic and extrinsic organizational crises.

A good example of a critical incident would be large scale rioting of the type, which took place during the Los Angeles riots of 1992.[2] A crisis is an event that exceeds our capacity, ability, or resources (CAR) to respond effectively. More generally, a crisis, in turn, is less severe in nature than a full-blown disaster. A disaster presumes the large-scale damage of infrastructure and loss of life, often associated with natural events such as earthquakes, hurricanes, flooding, and fires [5]. Unfortunately, some individuals conflate these different concepts. The list below details the core features and challenges that arise during a crisis and disaster event. It should come as no surprise that there is a significant degree of overlap between these elements and those of effective response presented elsewhere in this chapter.

2.2 The core features defining a crisis or disaster

1. A threat which manifests itself unexpectedly without notice
2. There is an urgent need for immediate decision-making
3. Available time for both decision-making and response is limited
4. Numerous requests for information flowing in both directions
5. Lack of organization, a sense of impending chaos
6. Stress factors continue to increase as event progresses
7. Standard operating procedures (SOPs) may no longer apply
8. Increased risk of reputational damage
9. Communications systems are challenged and difficult to manage (technical failures, overload, miscommunication...)
10. The "blame-game" starts
11. Difficulties relating to the maintenance of standard services

2.3 The crisis and disaster management process: Planning, preparation, response, and recovery

Crisis and disaster management is a cyclic process. The various stages include risk assessment, planning, preparation, mitigation and contingency, the response phase, a transition to recovery, and a final evaluation. The final evaluation phases, those of recovery and evaluation, are important, an importance that is sadly often underestimated or overlooked. Careful evaluation and incorporation of lessons

---

[2] The LA riots, sometimes referred to as the Rodney King riots, followed what was perceived as police brutality against Rodney King. During a traffic stop. King, a Black American was brutally assaulted. The subsequent repercussions were widespread and long-lasting and fostered deep-seated mistrust and contempt between the police and the Black community in the U.S.

Figure 2.
The crisis and disaster management cycle.

learned can enhance future resilience. Frequently and unfortunately neglected, in the sweeping wake of relief, which follows a major crisis or emergency event, are these vital final phases of the crisis and disaster management cycle. A prime example of this was witnessed during the military intervention in Iraq, where there was a clear failure to restore the rule of law. Soon following the invasion there was a lack of both coordinated international response and a concurrent failure to respect commitments. Sectarian conflict flared to alarming proportions. The result was anarchy, chaos, and bitter internecine Sunni-Shia factional violence on an unprecedented scale. Problems such as poor governance and widescale corruption still persist to this very day.

In **Figure 2**, one can visualize all the important phases of the crisis and disaster management response cycle. It is crucial to underscore the fact that within these cycles there are often other "mini cycles that need to be conducted as well." Thus, each phase of the cycle is simultaneously independent and interdependent.

2.4 Defining and characterizing risk: the first stage of CDMP

Formerly treated as an entirely separate field, risk and strategic risk management are now widely considered, by theoretical and applied research, as the first phase of the crisis and disaster management process. Pursiainen ([6], p. 9), for instance, recognizes the importance of risk management as a precondition for the successful response and resolution of a crisis or disaster event, in accordance with the crisis management cycle.

In order to measure a phenomenon, we must first be able to accurately define it. Risk may be considered to appear in two forms, the first category is risk which is known, has historical antecedents, and can be accurately measured. The second category of risk concerns a more ambiguous form that can be labeled as "uncertainty."

Uncertainty represents unforeseen or unimaginable events, referred to as "Black Swan events" (Taleb, 2008). Black Swan events are those events which by their unpredictable nature cannot be accurately forecast. A classic example was the multifaceted terrorist attacks of September 9, 2011. Another characteristic that often defines this type of event is that it appears more predictable that they appear more predictable than they were due to the application of hindsight. Another clearly illustrative example was the Fukushima Daiichi reactor meltdown in 2011.

Risk assessment then is (or at least should be) the *first phase* of the crisis and disaster management cycle. The definition of risk, nevertheless, remains elusive. Increasingly organizations consider risk as a state, which provide both opportunities and hazards (threats) in equal measure. In this regard, organizations are considered as either risk averse (risk avoidant), or having a risk appetite (risk seeking), or a combination of these, depending upon their stance and outlook. Pursiainen ([6], pp. 23-26) further underscores the difference between the historically based and measurable concept of risk from that of unmeasurable uncertainty, or unforeseen and unimagined risk.

The initial phase, that of risk assessment, is undertaken prior to planning and preparation. Before we can begin to develop plans and prepare to deal with various threats, we need first to identify, analyze, and evaluate those specific hazards. A risk matrix or risk register, such as the simplified one presented below in **Table 1**, is used to perform this operation.

Please be aware that risk matrices exist in a wide variety of models ranging from overly complex computational models based upon qualitative and quantitative evaluations, or a combination of these. The one presented here is easy to visualize, understand, configure, and apply. When calculating risk we are seeking, once again balance the probability of a critical event with the eventual consequences it may produce. There are also several ways to gauge these characteristics independently. Thus, probability may be gauged on a scale ranging from highly unlikely, to unlikely, possible, probable, and certain, with increasing degrees of certitude. Likewise, consequences may range from negligible, to moderate, critical, and catastrophic, once again in increasing degrees of importance.

The above matrix was developed by the author and employs a simple numerical scale of evaluation, which ranges from the least probable event, with a numerical factor of 1 multiplied by the lowest degree of consequence also with a numerical value of 1. Thus, multiplying the two values we obtain the lowest score (1). For the other values, we use the same method of multiplying the probability times the consequence. Thus, on the high end, one finds the highest probability (certain) with a value of 5. This is multiplied

PROBABILITY	IMPACT				
	Negligible 1	Minor 2	Moderate 3	Critical 4	Catastrophic 5
Certain 5	M 5	M 10	H 15	H 20	H 25
Probable 4	M 4	M 8	M 12	H 16	H 20
Possible 3	L 3	M 6	M 9	M 12	H 15
Improbable 2	L 2	L 4	M 6	M 8	M 10
Highly Unlikely 1	L 1	L 2	M 3	M 4	M 5

Matrix Scale 1-4 = Low; 5 – 12 = Medium; over 12 = High

Table 1.
A simplified risk matrix.

by the greatest consequence (catastrophic) also with a value of 5, producing a maximal risk rating of 25. In this way, the two criteria may be easily evaluated according to their significance. The colors were designed employing a standardized, green-amber-red, traffic signal pattern as per many similar examples in the literature. Green represents minimal threat, yellow a moderate threat, and red a threat of a significant hazard.

Once this process is complete and we are aware of the possible threats we face, we can then move on with the next two stages, which consist of *planning and preparation*. If the importance of the planning and preparation phases are not sufficiently emphasized and supported, not only will the personnel fail to develop a crisis management culture, but also the other subsequent stages of the cycle will be left wanting as well.

There are two clearly defining formulas, which help us define risk. The first is R = p x c, or probability x consequences will provide us with a relative estimation of risk incurred. The second formula defines and speaks to the confluence of three factors, whereby vulnerabilities + Assets + Threats = Risk or V + A + T = R. All three elements must be reunited for risk to manifest itself.

Assets are what is at risk, and represent what we are trying to protect and what is important to us (for instance, family friends, material possessions, wealth, and infrastructure). One category often overlooked when defining assets is that of intangible assets, such as knowledge. Knowledge and knowledge management (KM) are key resources and contribute to the long-term viability of any public service organization. *Vulnerabilities* represent weaknesses or gaps in our security or resilience, and finally, *threats* exploit our vulnerabilities in order to damage or destroy our assets. You must have all three for a threat to exist: no assets= no risk, just as no vulnerabilities or threats also = no (or limited) risk.

One critical point to bear in mind here is that there is no such thing as 0% risk. No matter how marginal it may be, there is always some degree of risk present. Every activity we undertake in life carries a risk, and the difference is that we assume those risks following a cost/benefit, or rational choice analysis and assigning them with relative priorities. The cost/benefits analysis is, however, not always entirely rational, as we shall see.

According to ISO 31000 [7], an organization can establish risk assessment through constant communication and consultation, after identifying the context of the risk through three core phases. These include *risk identification*, *risk analysis,* and *risk evaluation*. Subsequent to this is the development of the risk treatment plan (the method by which we intend to reduce the risk). We constantly monitor and evaluate the risk treatment plan for any eventual revision [7].

The three principal stages involved in the organizational risk treatment plan include the principles, the framework, and the actual processes themselves. In public service organizations, these elements need to be clearly defined and aligned according to the mission, values, and long-term goals of the organization. Risk management can never be a simple add-on or afterthought. If it is to be effective, it must be adopted by the entire organization with proactive support from the executive. It is also important to clarify that when evaluating risk there exist both intrinsic and extrinsic objectives, the risk to the organization itself, and the risks involved in its crisis and disaster response framework.

2.5 Planning, preparation, mitigation, and contingency

While no two crises or disasters are ever the same, it is worth bearing in mind that there do exist common denominators between various events. It is, therefore, possible to plan, prepare, train, exercise, and practice that level. The total lack of training and practice will offer a response that is equally inadequate such as that we witnessed during hurricane Katrina. Additionally, preplanning and preparation for the strategic allocation of resources and the prepositioning of emergency facilities can offer a tremendous advantage to the organization when a crisis or disaster does occur.

The planning phase can be conducted using what is commonly referred to as the SWIFT technique, or the Strategic "what if" technique. This is a "Delphi, method, whereby a group, composed of both pertinent stakeholders and subject matter experts (SME's), sits together, and poses questions concerning risks faced by the organization. The use of keywords, such as "people" and "infrastructure" will help to define the core parameters of concern. The organization pares down the list to a manageable number of hazards by selecting only the most relevant and realistic threats facing the organization. Once the threats have been adequately identified, defined, and evaluated, a plan regarding pre-event mitigation and post-event contingency countermeasures to be taken can then be developed and implemented. It is also during the planning to preparation phase that appropriate training and exercise cycles are also developed.

2.6 Response phase

Once the threat manifests itself, or the critical incident exceeds the capacity, abilities, or resources of the organization, there is the need for interoperability (see JESIP chapter on decision making and a unified response to the given situation)[3] [8]. We develop the guidelines of this process in the planning and preparation phase of the crisis and disaster management cycle. This includes private-public partnerships (PPP's), as well as collaborating with alternative stakeholders such as non-governmental agencies (NGO's), charitable organizations, volunteer groups, and the public. Effective response to a critical incident, crisis, or disaster event is primordial for safeguarding organizational reputation.

2.6.1 Interoperability and the C7 doctrine

Interoperability has been framed within the context of inter-agency communications. It is the opinion of this research, however, that such a limited application is both counterproductive and counterintuitive. Indeed, the concept of interoperability, as envisioned in this chapter relates to what has been referred to as the C7 Doctrine.

The C7 doctrine is a combination of four core elements (C4): two leadership variables (C2) and community involvement. C4 includes communication, cooperation, coordination, and collaboration. In passing, it is useful to bear in mind that cooperation and collaboration are the distinct approaches. Cooperation indicates two or more agencies working together, while collaboration, a much deeper concept, relates to two or more agencies working together with a common goal or objective. The reference to C2 concerns command and control, essential for the proper preparation, response, and recovery from crisis and disaster events. Without proper lines of command and control, all phases of operations will be negatively impacted. Finally, and by no means, less important is the element of community.

Another integral part of achieving optimal interoperability lies in the development of a common training framework or CTF. Agencies that work together on a regular basis and those that may eventually be called upon to assist in a large-scale event need to have the proper cooperation and collaboration that only combined training protocols can provide.

[3] https://www.jesip.org.uk/wp-content/uploads/2022/03/JESIP_Joint-Doctrine_Guide_APRIL2022.pdf.

One enormous advantage to such an approach lies in the possibility to draw from a wide well of experiential and organizational knowledge. A joint response, when properly coordinated, is a more effective response by any measure. Immediately we tend to think of police, fire, and medical; however, there are a host of other agencies that need to grasp and understand the joint operational framework. The axiom: fail to plan=plan to fail comes to mind. Thus, stakeholders, both public and private, can contribute to the enhanced preparedness and resilience of the community.

Private organizations and local businesses can be incorporated into private-public partnerships, or PPPs, and other stakeholders such as military units, border control, maritime and aviation services, as well as various corporate entities, businesses, NGOs, and community and religious leaders should all be incorporated and encouraged to participate in plans for effective preparation, response, and recovery aspects of a potential disaster. At least fifty-seven deaths occurred during the freak Texas snowstorm of 2021 [9]. Better preparedness and visionary training through the adoption of a multi-stakeholder approach could have help reduce the impact significantly. One needless death is always one too many.

2.6.2 Elements of effective crisis response

1. Maintaining reputational integrity

2. Sound planning and preparedness

3. Solid leadership

4. Effective and timely communications

5. Strategic, well-organized interagency collaboration

6. Strategic resource allocation

7. Successful operational tactics, and

8. Post-crisis evaluation and learning to improve from any errors committed along the way

2.6.3 Cascading events

Crisis and disaster events do not always occur in isolation. It often happens that multiple events take place simultaneously, or a single event serves as a force multiplier. They may precipitate and trigger a complex series of interrelated and unforeseen events rapidly playing off one another in random succession, resulting in far greater damage and negative consequences. Such compound events of course create a greater economic and social impact. Cascading events also call for increased resources, logistics, and personnel as part of an effective response. Noticeably clear examples of cascading events, sometimes referred to as the domino effect, can be witnessed during many crises or disasters. The negative impacts may be immediate, or they can be described as long shadow events. That is, events with a rapid start and quick conclusion, but which, nevertheless, result in long term effects, such as in the case of the Fukushima Daiichi nuclear reactor incident in 2011.

Recent research indicates that the Fukushima Daiichi Nuclear Power Plant released particles containing radioactive cesium, Cs137—one of the more common fission products by the nuclear fission of uranium-235, during the 2011 nuclear disaster in addition to trace amounts of plutonium 241 as well other radioactive isotopes [10, 11]. The half-life of these materials are 30 and 50 years, respectively. As Fukushima occurred only 11 years ago, we are still in hot water, so to speak. When considering the gravity of this event one can compare it with Chernobyl as both events were rated as level 7 disasters rated level 7 on the International Nuclear and Radiological Event Scale by IAEA.

Recently, on July 21, 2022, the Japanese government admitted their failed decontamination policies with regard to effectively dealing with the disaster. This resulted in the environmentally catastrophic decision to release the contaminated Fukushima Daichi waters into the Pacific Ocean. According to the best research estimates and projections, the contaminated waters are slated to enter the East China Sea, and nearby South Korean waters as early as 7 months following the release. Levels of all radioactive materials were well above international levels, even when accounting for previous nuclear weapons testing.

Other long shadow events with enduring consequences can be witnessed in the case of the attacks on the World Trade Center in 2001, or the more recent COVID-19 pandemic that resulted in long-lasting political, economic, social, technological, legal, and environmental (PESTLE) upheaval. Any crisis or disaster event is, therefore, capable of producing short term, long-term negative consequences, or any combination of these in tandem.

2.7 Recovery and evaluation phase

Often overlooked and given short shrift, the recovery phase is just as important, if not more important in some respects, than the actual intervention and response. This is the result of a normal human reaction. The high-stress levels calling for immediate action and decision making incurred as a feature of the response phase dissipate. Relief of having survived the worst subsumes thoughts of recovery once the danger has passed is but a memory.

There should always be a formal handover of authority between those responsible for the response phase and those dealing with recovery from the aftermath of an incident. The reason for this formal handover of authority and responsibility is quite obvious. Those concerned with the recovery process require a different skill set than those responding to the same event. This includes different formation and training. On a purely practical level, those who responded to a major event would find themselves taxed and overburdened should they be required to continue without respite. There is an additional symbolic aspect to this handover, and that is the aspect of passing from the phase of active response to one of active recovery. It is precisely this aspect that often leads to organizations neglecting the importance of the recovery phase as relief settles in and the crisis becomes an undesirable past event.

It is absolutely essential to incorporate the public as an integral component of the recovery process. This was evident during the Thai Cave Crisis, where the authorities established a specifically designated area and support services for the relatives of the children.[4] The Thai cave crisis took place in Thailand's Chiang Rai province. Twelve

[4] Seeforinstance:https://www.thenational.ae/world/thai-cave-rescue-everything-we-know-so-far-1.747347

young boys accompanied by their sports coach decided to explore some caves and became trapped in a small, isolated pocket inside with no clear exit. The group risked drowning due to rapidly rising seasonal flooding. Their eventual rescue was a tale of courage, ingenuity, and international cooperation. As with the other two core features of the crisis and disaster management cycle, planning and preparation, and response, recovery too has the same core components of preparation, response, evaluation, and reconfiguration (as necessary).

3. Public service organizations (PSOs)

3.1 Seeking a cohesive approach

Despite the fact that this chapter presents a cohesive approach to the Crisis and Disaster Management Process (CDMP), it is, nevertheless, impossible to provide the level of detail this topic deserves.[5] Here, we are examining a selective approach to CDMP and how it pertains to PSOs.

It was only following a significant rise of social, technological, and natural disasters and their accompanying devastating impacts, during the 1980s, that risk assessment, health and safety culture, and crisis and disaster management eventually made their entry into the public service and not-for-profit sectors. The challenges relating to critical events have become more numerous, more widespread, and increasingly complex. For instance, technology has become a complex system of systems. Processes such as nuclear plant operation have become so complex that they surpass human capability and often require oversight by other systems such as industrial control systems (ICS) or supervisory control and data acquisition (SCADA).

Public service organizations, and policing agencies in particular, are currently facing new challenges and taking on responsibilities that were hitherto not a part of their purview. This has led to a more diversified approach to risk management, often referred to as *risk governance*. Whereas risk had previously been contained at the organizational level, today the reach and impact of various crises and disasters are far more diverse and include a more global perspective. Issues such as natural disasters, transnational-armed conflict, transnational organized criminal activity, (henceforth TOCA), trafficking (in persons, arms, fauna, stolen art, and artifacts), cybercrime, terrorism, and public health order are now often the concerns of police agencies at the international level, with domestic repercussions.

It is essential that organizations have an appropriate vision and terminology when dealing with risk and the CDMP. When speaking of the recovery process, for example, the term most frequently encountered in the literature is "business continuity." Public service entities are uniquely different from their public sector counterparts and their enterprise risk management approach (ERM). Terms such as "service continuity," "service maintenance," or "service delivery," "would be far more appropriate to describe this process." Descriptive terminology is important in fostering a clear understanding. In order for public service organizations (PSOs) to accept and fully take ownership of the crisis and disaster management process, they must have that process and its associated terminology appropriately tailored to their needs.

5 For a more in-depth understanding there is a complementary suggested reading list provided at the end of the chapter.

3.2 Reputation (R) and Trust (T) as integral assets of PSOs

It is worth underscoring here the significance of the threat posed to organizational reputation. One of the principal, and most important, assets of any public service organization is its reputation. There are countless incidents where severe reputational damage negatively affected public confidence and trust and even resulted in political and social upheaval due to excessive police repression. Pertinent examples include the 1991, LAPD beating of Rodney King incident [12], or the Danziger Bridge murders (a case study presented in this chapter), to name but two. More recently, we may cite overly aggressive police responses during the COVID-19 pandemic. This relationship may be presented as the "Big R = Big T" formula, whereby an organization's *reputation* is contingent upon public *trust* and conversely, public trust is founded upon the reputation of the organization. In the advent of flawed, inadequate, improper, unjust, or overly aggressive responses by a public service organization, there will be a corresponding loss of reputational credibility. This, in turn, leads directly to a decline in public trust in said organization. Thus, the concepts of reputation and trust exercise a reciprocal relationship.

3.3 PSO responsibilities during crisis and disaster events

The police and other PSO's have significant and challenging duties even under the most normal conditions. During critical incidents and in times of crisis and disaster, unsurprisingly, challenges and responsibilities are compounded. In addition to their normal fare of providing and maintaining safety, security, and public order, responders must cope with issues such as interoperability, crisis communication, the effective allocation of limited resources, mass evacuation, dealing with the disruption of and damage to public utilities, provision of emergency shelter, psychological support, responding to rioting and prohibiting looting, providing emergency medical treatment, and conducting victim identification and much more. All these various roles and responsibilities need to be considered when developing an action plan during the planning and preparation phase.

As far as law enforcement is concerned, there are five core functions relating to policing during a crisis or natural disaster. The first four were cited back by Will. C. Kennedy [13], and these guiding precepts, nevertheless, remain immutable to the present day. A fifth function has been added here:

1. Crowd control and traffic flow

2. Protection of life and property

3. Search and rescue

4. Warning and evacuation

5. Preventing looters

It is unfortunately only in the wake of recent disasters, such as that of Hurricane Katrina, that there has been increased awareness about the roles and responsibilities of the police during events such as natural disasters. While the above five-outlined principles are obvious and make clear sense, some of their characterizations may not be so straightforward.

Subsumed under these guiding principles, we might also consider, more specifically, related functions. These include establishing command centers, commandeering, organizing, and assuring logistic and communication support, treating, and transporting the sick and injured, loss prevention and anti-looting, prisoner relocation, establishing areas of safe passage, or assuring the safety of other responders including the more obvious fire, medical, and rescue personnel but also less obvious personnel such as volunteers and public utilities, among others. Another important concern is striking a balance among crime fighting, service maintenance, and the actual disaster response. In many, if not all, cases, the first two concerns become secondary in light of disaster response and survival priorities.

The consensus is that the first three hours following a disaster are most crucial. We might logically refer to these and the CDMP "golden hours." The relative evaluation of damage to infrastructure and the loss of life should occur during this immediate response phase and the public appropriately informed. This helps to curtail misinformation and the spread of rumors and contributes to effective communication management The Hurricane Katrina case study is a classic one which officers and other crisis, and disaster management personnel should acquaint themselves with. It offers pertinent examples of how not to conduct a crisis management event, and it would, therefore, be remiss, to overlook the important lessons learned from that particular disaster. Our specific case study presented at the end of this chapter will deal with just once incident during these events—the Danziger Bridge shootings [14], described later in this chapter.

3.3.1 Policing aspect

When questioned as to the responsibilities of the police during such events, most individuals would respond that the primary function of the police is the assurance of public safety, the provision of public security, and the maintenance of public order. Increasingly, however, the functions fulfilled, the responsibilities held, and the services provided by police and other public service agencies have shifted dramatically. Police leadership and their respective agencies are currently being tasked do more with less. This infers that during a crisis or a disaster event their ability to maintain normal services is disrupted and what service is provided may be inadequate or subpar.

While all the previously mentioned imperatives certainly still apply, a host of newer and even greater challenges, such as public incivility and negative social dynamics, has compounded former responsibilities. This is particularly true in light of technological advances such as the Internet, digital communications, and the advent of social media, all of which hold both promise and challenge in equal measure. This chapter will explore various aspects of crisis and disaster management, through an optic of police responsibility during crisis and disaster, leadership and interoperability during crisis and disaster, and crisis communications as they pertain to policing in the twenty-first century.

4. Public service failures

4.1 Hurricane Katrina: a spectacular public service failure

The research will adopt Hurricane Katrina, as a case study template for crisis and disaster management in policing, and explore one particular incident during that event, that of the Danziger bridge shooting, for reflective analysis. The Danziger Bridge incident occurred early in the morning of September 4, 2005. This was six days following the arrival of Hurricane Katrina. Officers from the New Orleans Police Department (NOPD) scrambled in response to what was allegedly a call from another officer who had been fired upon. Two civilians were shot dead, and four others seriously injured. Later investigation revealed that none of the victims had committed any crime, nor were they armed. To make matters worse the original investigation was flawed by misreporting and the planting of false evidence. The trust in the police eroded and public cooperation vanished as a result of this incident. We shall take a further, in-depth look at this event later in this chapter.

During Hurricane Katrina, a large number of officers failed to respect their obligations to report for duty, fleeing the city with their families instead, as Benjamin Sims [15] attests to the fact that "Hundreds of police officers resigned or simply walked off the job, two committed suicide, and those who remained were severely demoralized and under extreme stress" [15]. Such unforeseen dynamics often alter the response and exceed both expectations and contingency plans. Strong visionary leadership, creative and flexible thinking, and organizational improvisation can usually overcome them [15]. Of course, one of the most key features related to crisis and disaster emergency response for PSO's is effective interoperability and effective interagency collaboration, something that was severely missing during the Hurricane Katrina disaster. Subsumed under the acronym C7, there are seven principal concerns while dealing with any crisis or disaster event; these are Command and Control (C2) Cooperation, Communication, Collaboration and Coordination (C4), and Community. These are covered in detail in a later section of this chapter.

Katrina represents an excellent case study, since the primary function of case studies is for learning and avoiding the mistakes that others have made, rather than merely assessing successful responses. The importance of case studies, therefore, is not what went right, rather what went wrong and how public service organizations, such as the police, can avoid similar errors in the future, while incorporating lessons learned into their future action plans.

During Hurricane Katrina, the New Orleans Police Department lost this valuable window of opportunity in S&R (search and rescue) operations, bringing close to three hundred of its own officers to safety. According to Cha [16], the total number of officers who showed up for work represented only around two-thirds of the entire force, while Anderson [17], reported that following the events of Hurricane Katrina, "sixty officers resigned, forty-five were fired [plus an additional 6 civilian employees], and two officers committed suicide" [15]. Other sources cite different figures where they state ninety-one officers resigned and 228 investigated for disappearing from their assigned duties, and Baum [18] reported that more than a 150 officers were eventually fired or left the department, of their own accord, after failing to perform during the crisis. Another 40 having been placed under investigation. In the end, according to Scharf and Phillippi [14] a staggering number of officers, more than 200, who walked away from their, in total, were either fired or disciplined. Many of those would did walker away from their responsibilities were younger, less experienced, and felt overwhelmed by events according to Treaster [19]. There were 1,833-recorded deaths, related to the disaster, in total [20].

Regardless of the exact numbers, such figures would represent a heavy toll in human capital for any public service organization. Additionally, as Eunjung Cha [16] noted, "In the days before the hurricane, the police force numbered 1750. After Katrina, officials could account for only a few more than 1200." No one knows whether the missing are dead, injured, or just could not face the horror of the work. There were critical external drivers involved: poor training, a lack of disaster resilience, failed mitigation, and the absence of any meaningful contingency planning, all of which contributed to the disastrous response. The failed response was also the culmination of a number of factors ranging from rampant corruption, failed preparations, and inadequate organizational management for ineffective and inefficient provision of shelter and evacuation, widespread negligence, poor leadership, and especially organizational paralysis in the face of disaster [21].

If the storm front and other factors were not bad enough, they were compounded by backed up sewers, a lack of running water, approximately 2,000 dead littering the streets, widespread theft in vacated homes, and looting of shops being conducted by wayward citizens. A limited number of rogue officers were also involved in the looting themselves, raising the pertinent idiomatic question "*Quis custodiet ipsos custodes*?" [22] (In other words, who will guard the guardians?) The significance of officers joining in the looting led to the perception that the rule of law had collapsed. Such a condition can easily tip a situation into anomie, as it did in this instance. During a crisis or disaster event, perception frequently becomes more powerful a predictor of behavior than fact. In addition to these various elements, there was a failure at both the state and federal levels to understand the complexity, depth, and importance of the disaster and to organize effective assistance in its wake.

4.2 Danziger bridge case study: does reputation matter?

Date of event: September 4, 2005. **Description of event:** Six NOPD officers, none of them in uniform, responded to a report of officers under fire. They commandeered a Budget rental truck. They left the vehicle firing their weapons. There was no evidence, according to federal prosecutors of police having been under fire at the time. They were in fact firing upon unarmed civilians seeking food and medicine in the wake of Hurricane Katrina.

Death and injury: The officers killed two civilians and injured four others. The officers shot Ronald Madison, a forty-year-old mentally disabled man, in the back and repeatedly kicked as he lay dying. James Brisette, the other fatality was only 17-year-old [14].

Attempted cover-up: In an attempt to exculpate, the seven officers indicted on July 6, 2005, Homicide detective Arthur "Archie" Kaufman, appointed as lead investigator, attempted to conceal evidence and falsified reports, while NOPD Lieutenant Michael Lohman planted a personal unregistered weapon (called a "ham sandwich") near the scene in order to justify the shootings.

Prosecution results: Seven officers under indictment. State charges vacated in August 2008. Federal prosecutors indicted four of the officers on murder charges on July 12, 2010. Five officers found guilty on August 5, 2011. Hefty sentences ranging between six and sixty-five years were handed down. On September 17, 2013, a retrial ordered based upon prosecutorial misconduct. On April 20, 2016, the five defendants plead guilty to reduced charges and receive reduced sentences, and on December 19, 2016, four civil lawsuits also resulted in a settlement for the families and victims of this event.

Consequences: Severely damaged reputation and negative impact on public confidence in the police. Compounded and magnified other concurrent police misadventures such as unauthorized commandeering of luxury Cadillacs, looting by a limited number of officers, and 228 officers failing to report.

4.3 Ethics and responsibility: a crisis wrapped inside a disaster

As we have seen, there was an inadequate and failed response on the part of local, state, and federal government in the wake of Hurricane Katrina. The natural disaster, compounded by failed response on the human side, sullied the reputation of anyone involved and particularly that of the New Orleans Police Department (NOPD). Hurricane Katrina compounded NOPDs already previously weak and tarnished reputation. It took a devastating direct hit with the Danziger Bridge shootings

4.4 Lessons

4.4.1 Crisis communications

As might be expected from the preceding remarks on Hurricane Katrina, there was also a total collapse and failure of the crisis communications network and associated systems. Communications are a core requirement for PSOs to function effectively. From delivery of services to cross-hierarchy communications, the ability to transmit pertinent and timely information cannot be underestimated. Additionally, in a large-scale disaster event such as that of Hurricane Katrina, it became painfully obvious that failed communications not only hampered rescue operations but also severely restricted and reduced all interagency efforts as well.

During Hurricane Karina, the entire electrical system and telephone exchange—both wired and wireless, became inoperable. This of course resulted in a lack of computer access to the Internet, with the consequent lack of ability to issue public warnings and information, such as evacuation plans. When the Hurricane made landfall, high winds knocked over emergency response radio towers, rendering the 800 MHz emergency radio system for the entire state of Louisiana inoperable for a period of several days, while flooding washed out most of the backup generators [15].

Additionally, the fact that one of two police officers who committed suicide was the public information officer, or the PIO, certainly did not bode well for the crisis communication plan and cast a dark shadow over those feeble efforts. These events were the direct result of poor foresight, inadequate planning, and a total absence of any effective mitigation strategies. All commanders had been distributed detailed hurricane response plan in 2004, but this remained untouched and lay unused gathering dust on bookshelves. In addition to these numerous problems, both Mayor C. Ray Nagin and Superintendent of police Edwin P. Compass added to the reigning panic and confusion while appearing on Oprah on September 6, 2005, with poorly informed, inaccurate, and misplaced announcements that

> *"We had little babies in there, some of the little babies getting raped." Mayor C. Ray Nagin concurred: "They have people standing out there, have been in that frickin' Superdome for five days watching dead bodies, watching hooligans killing people, raping people." [15, 23].*

The ill-fated Convention Center and the Superdome housed approximately 20,000 people per structure, and many huddled in deplorable conditions lacking fresh water, toilets, or air-conditioning in the stifling heat. Given the fact that there was only a single homicide recorded at the Convention Center, one can only surmise that their ill-conceived strategy was to create a shock effect designed to receive immediate and substantial federal support. The unfettered media also contributed to the widespread veil of fear and panic by speculating and promoting such unsubstantiated rumors as well. Such cases bear witness to the difference between responsible reporting and freedom of the press.

In *Policing Major Events* Hanser et al. [11] discuss the role of the Federal emergency center (FEMA) in Baton Rouge, and they monitored the path of the hurricane but over 100.000 people were still in New Orleans with no means of transport. The police in New Orleans faced difficulties, with 150 police officers abandoning their positions. There was duplication of response efforts between New Orleans Police (NOPD) and FEMA. This clearly indicates a lack of effective communication and coordinated response. Communications were difficult, and the communication systems had been damaged. The violence that ensued after the hurricane was subsequently accompanied by in widespread looting.

The comprehensive U.S. House of Representatives report, "A Failure of Initiative" [24] highlighted the fact that "As Hurricane Katrina approached New Orleans, and the devastation started, it was immediately evident that the concept of unity of command and mutual cooperation had become fragmented." Much of this chaos was a result of the unforeseen scale of damage incurred in the early hours of the hurricane. The report continued "Local governments' command and control was often paralyzed by the complete destruction of their entire emergency management infrastructure" (p. 184). This completely contradicts the logic advanced by Wachtendorf [25], who asserts that organizations create sense making in the face of uncertainty by drawing on plans. The disaster plans for New Orleans were in place, but they gathered dust on a shelf. The same report observed that despite the fact that the Department of Homeland Security (DHS), The Federal Emergency Management Agency (FEMA), and other government bodies had conducted extensive planning and training for events such as this, there was, nevertheless, a catastrophic breakdown in the emergency response in New Orleans.

The conclusions of the report by the U.S. House of Representatives [24] were abundantly clear, emphasizing that "This lack of coordinated response led to ineffective rescue, recovery, relief operations, and communications (media) strategies." Local, state, and federal organizations failed to properly coordinate and control in any meaningful way. Operations such as search and rescue, providing food and drinking water, evacuations, and other essential elements of any major rescue and recovery response, were entirely inadequate. One of the unintended consequences of the evacuation of some 250,000 people to Houston in Texas was the number of people on parole from prison (estimated at between 1,300 and 1,700 people) and the gang members who took advantage of the situation to escape to Texas. This shortsightedness has had negative post-disaster security repercussions.

4.4.2 The media

Traditional media, sometimes referred to as "analog," covers things such as printed material, newspapers, and other forms of non-digital communications.

Traditional media is still an important source of information and communication for several reasons:

- Traditional media is favored by marginalized groups who may not benefit from other forms of communication

- Traditional media can be effective and complementary when digital sources, such as during Hurricane Katrina, are knocked out

- Failing to incorporate traditional news sources into crisis reporting can backfire on organizations and open the door to criticism and reputational damage. Public service organizations may lose the narrative and become victim to disinformation, misinformation, and distortion.

4.4.3 Leadership during crisis and disaster

Powerful events call for powerful leadership and decision making. During a critical incident or crisis event, there are two fundamental requirements: an organization to respond and a leader to direct their efforts. While there exist countless theories defining leadership, there is no one clear and decisive framework that applies to all leaders in all situations at all times. Leadership is one skill that escapes analysis and definition. A leader who proves exemplary under normal circumstances may crack under the strain and pressure of a major crisis or disaster and fail to rise to the challenge. One fact remains certain is that critical incidents, crises, and disasters evaluate the mettle of even the strongest leaders. This is where the concept of teamwork and the allocation of responsibility also come into play. An effective leader never attempts to deal with a crisis event single handed, he or she knows they must be able rely upon well trained and trusted subordinates.

What then are the specific characteristics that a leader needs to exhibit when faced with a crisis or disaster event? Accountability, integrity, and trustworthiness are indispensable. Failure to exhibit these traits and set an example for subordinates will have a negative impact on the entire organization. Leaders need to be visionary and flexible, and able to change and adapt plans according to the ever-changing and challenging circumstances they face. They must be able to rise to the occasion and make decisions rather than prevaricate and hesitate during the decision-making process. Finally, the leader needs to accept and assume responsibility for their decisions.

Most police leaders have enough knowledge and experience that should they make a "wrong" decision such a decision will have negligible effects. At the end of the day, a wrong decision is preferable to no decision whatsoever. Leaders must be able to offer strong affirmative direction and still be open to suggestions and feedback from subordinates. Finally, during a crisis and disaster event, leaders will both delegate authority and responsibility, as well as sharing authority and responsibility with interagency partners.

5. Conclusion and recommendations

The entire spectrum of the CDMP has been addressed in this chapter. This will serve as an introduction to those who are unfamiliar with the process and as a refresher for those who have mastered the associated skills involved. Responding to critical incidents such as crises and disasters requires not only dedication and motivation, but also continuous monitoring and pre-crisis training.

A crisis or disaster event can, and often does, occur without warning; however, in those instances when there is advanced warning public service organizations must be well-trained and ready to respond at a moment's notice. Today's public service organizations are overwhelmed, underfunded, and understaffed. They are forced to do more with less. In order to maintain an adequate level of service, it is essential that they learn past lessons from different case studies to avoid falling into the same traps and committing the same errors. It is essential to maintain a high sense of purpose and professionalism despite the increasing pressure and obstacles to organizational performance.

Emergency, crisis, and disaster management are but one of the numerous challenges for which officers and departments must be prepared. All too often crisis and disaster management begins with the best of intentions, but momentum and commitment are quickly lost in the struggle to balance other, more immediate issues. It is incumbent upon the leadership to create and maintain a culture of risk and crisis preparedness lest they fall into the turmoil similar to that witnessed during Hurricane Katrina.

This imperative entails a number of important recommendations and steps to be introduced. Prominently figured among these required adaptations are adequate training based on common training framework (CTF) and education, proper logistical support for the effective and timely allocation of limited resources, robust interagency collaboration, and a visionary leadership executive that leads by example. Dedicating a portion training and awareness on CDMP to PSOs on a regular basis is primordial for successful response and resolution of crisis and disaster events. Merely having a plan in place is not enough. Even the best plan in the world is useless if, like in the case of Hurricane Katrina, it remains on a shelf-gathering dust.

Being aware and taking advantage of new technological developments, such as artificial intelligence (AI), unmanned aerial vehicles (UAVs), early warning systems (EWSs), and computer modeling in conjunction with new life-saving advances, will contribute to the effectiveness of responding organizations. It is highly recommended that governments adopt a more proactive approach to fostering such research and development (R&D) in the field of CDMP. This will lower the burden of strained PSOs while increasing their ability to respond more effectively.

Citizens and the private sector must be made aware and informed of their roles and the importance of their efforts in conjunction with public service organizations. It was never a feasible assumption that PSOs would take full responsibility during times of crisis and disaster, and in the current challenging environment, it is even less the case.

Hopefully, the information and insights provided in this chapter will contribute to a better understanding and awareness of the importance of crisis and disaster preparedness as it pertains to public service organizational management during critical periods of crisis and disaster while providing room for expanded development and research in this critical area.

Suggested reading

General Reading

Barton L, Luecke R, Barton L. Crisis Management: Mastering the Skills to Prevent Disasters (Harvard Business Essentials). 1st ed. Cambridge, MA: Harvard University Press; 2004

Risk Management

Aven T. Implications of Black Swans to the foundations and pratice of risk assessment and managment. Reliability Engineering and system Safety. 2015;**134**:83-91

Ball DJ, Watt J. Further thoughts on the utility of risk matrices. Risk Analysis. 2013;**33**(11):2068-2078

Bao C et al. Comparison of different methods to design risk matrices from the perspective of applicability. Information Technology and Quantitative Management (ITQM 2017). 2017;**122**:455-462

Cox LA. What's wrong with risk matrices? Risk Analysis. 2008;*28*(2): 497-512. DOI: 10.1111/j.1539-6924. 2008.01030.x

Pursiainen C. The Crisis Managment Cycle. 1st ed. Oxon: Routledge; 2018

Taleb NN. The Black Swan: Second Edition: The Impact of the Highly Improbable: With a new section: "On Robustness and Fragility". 2nd ed. London: Penguin Books Ltd.; 2008

Disaster Research

El-Tawil S, Aguirre B. Search and rescue in collapsed structures: Engineering and social science aspects. Disasters. 2010;**34**(4):1084-1101

Flage R, Aven T. Emerging risk—Conceptual definition and a relation to balck swan type of events. Reliabilty Engineering and System Safety. 2015;**144**:61-67

Quarantelli EL. Organizational Behavior in Disasters and Implications For Disaster Planning. Newark, DE: Disaster Research Center; 1985

Wachtendorf T. Improvising 9/11: Organiationsl improvisation following the world trade center [doctoral thesis]. Newark, Delaware: Univerity of Delaware; 2004

Policing During Crisis and Disaster Events

Kennedy W. The Police Department in Natural Disaster Situations. Delaware: The Disaster Research Center, Departmentof Sociology, University of Delaware; 1969

Crisis Communications

Fink S. Crisis Communications: The Definitive Guide to Managing the Message. 1st ed. New York: McGraw-Hill Education; 2013

Seeger MW, Sellnow TL, Ulmer RR. Effective Crisis Communication: Moving From Crisis to Opportunity. 4th ed. Thousand Oaks, Calif: SAGE Publications, Inc; 2017

Interoperability

Wilkinson B, Cohen-Hatton SR, Honey RC. Decision-making in multi-agency groups at simulated major incident emergencies: In situ analysis of adherence to UK doctrine. Journal of Contingencies and Crisis Management. 2019:306-316

Leadership in Times of Crisis and Disaster

Boin A, t'Hart P, Stern E, Sundelius B. The Politics of Crisis Management: Public leadership under pressure. 4th ed. Cambridge: Cambridge University Press; 2006

Hurricane Katrina Case Study

Baum D. Deluged: When Katrina hit, where were the polcie?. 2006 [Online].Available from: https://www.newyorker.com/magazine/2006/01/09/deluged.[Accessed: 15 July 2019]

Boin A, t'Hart P, Stern E, Sundelius B. The Politics of Crisis Management: Public leadership under pressure. 4th ed. Cambridge: Cambridge University Press; 2006

Breed, A. G., 2005. Immense Hurricane Roars Toward New Orleans. [Online]. Available from: http://wirednewyork.com/forum/archive/index.php/t-7147.html.[Accessed 7 August 2019].

Carr D, More Horrible Than Truth: News Reports. 2005 [Online]. Available from: https://www.nytimes.com/2005/09/19/business/media/more-horrible-than-truth-news-reports.html.[Accessed 4 August 2019]

Cha A E. New Orleans Police Keep Public Trust, Private Pain. 2005 [Online]. Available from: https://www.washingtonpost.com/archive/politics/2005/09/12/new-orleans-police-keep-public-trust-private-pain/f539fa07-d7a1-4efa-b7ad-a68e6d9bd9a8/. [Accessed 6 August 2019].

Committe on Homelad Security and Governmental Affairs. Hurricane Katrina: A Nation Still Unprepared. Washington D.C.: U.S. Government Printing Office; 2006

Fink S. Five Days at Memorial: Life and Death in a Storm-Ravaged Hospital. 1st ed. New York: Crown; 2013

Public Broadcasting System. 2011. Behind the Danziger Bridge Shooting. Available from: Frontline: https://www.pbs.org/video/frontline-behind-the-danziger-bridge-shooting/

Select Bipartisan Committee to Investigate the Preparation for and the Response to Hurrican Katrina. A Failure of Initiative. Washington D.C.: U.S. Government Printing Office; 2006

Treaster J P. Law Officers, Overwhelmed, Are Quitting the Force. 2005. Available from: https://www.nytimes.com/2005/09/04/us/nationalspecial/law-officers-overwhelmed-are-quitting-the-force.html. [Accessed: 06 August 2019]

Treaster J B, DeSantis J. Storm and Crisis: The Police; With Some Now at Breaking Point, City's Officers Tell of Pain and Pressure. 2005. Available from: https://www.nytimes.com/2005/09/06/us/nationalspecial/police-officers-tell-ofpain-and-pressure.html. [Accessed: 4 July 2019]

Wiggington M P Jr. The New Orleans Police Emergency Reponse to Hurricane Katrina: A Case Study. University of Southern Mississippi, Hattiesburg: The University of Southern Mississippi. 2007. Available from: https://aquila.usm.edu/dissertations/1343. [Accessed: 28 July 2019]

The Danziger Bridge Shootings

Greene R. Shots on the Bridge: Police Violence and Cover-Up in the Wake of Katrina. Boston: Beacon Press; 2015

Youtube video clip: https://www.youtube.com/watch?v=m7t4dh3XsYg

Author details

James P. Welch
Policing and Security Department, Rabdan Academy, Abu Dhabi, UAE

*Address all correspondence to: doctorjamespwelch@outlook.com

References

[1] Kennedy W. The Police Department in Natural Disaster Situations. Delaware: The Disaster Research Center, Department of Sociology, University of Delaware; 1969

[2] Quarantelli EL. Organizational Behavior in Disasters and Implications for Disaster Planning. Newark, DE: Disaster Research Center; 1985

[3] Fink S. Crisis Communications: The Definitive Guide to Managing the Message. 1st ed. New York: McGraw-Hill Education; 2013. p. 7

[4] Boin A, t'Hart P, Stern E & Sundelius, B. The Politics of Crisis Management: Public leadership under pressure. 4th ed. Cambridge: Cambridge University Press; 2006

[5] El-Tawil S, Aguirre B. Search and rescue in collapsed structures: Engineering and social science aspects. Disasters. 2010;**34**(4):1084-1101

[6] Pursiainen C. The Crisis Management Cycle. 1st ed. Oxon: Routledge; 2018

[7] International Organization for Standardization. ISO 3100-2:2018 Risk Management Guidelines. Geneva: ISO; 2018

[8] Joint Emergency Services Interoperability Principles [JESIP], Joint Doctrine: The Interoperability Framework; Edition 3 (October 2021). 2021. Available from: https://www.jesip.org.uk/uploads/media/pdf/JESIP_Joint_Doctrine_Guide_OCT21.pdf and https://www.jesip.org.uk/wp-content/uploads/2022/03/JESIP_Joint-Doctrine_Guide_APRIL2022.pdf

[9] Sparber S. At Least 57 People Died in the Texas Winter Storm, Mostly from Hypothermia [Online]. 2021. Available from: https://www.texastribune.org/2021/03/15/texas-winter-storm-deaths/. [Accessed: 14 July 2022]

[10] Ewing R. Newly Discovered Particles Released During the Fukushima Daiichi Meltdowns. [Online]. 2021. Available from: https://fsi.stanford.edu/news/newly-discovered-particles-released-during-fukushima-daiichi-meltdowns. [Accessed: 28 September 2022]

[11] Hanser RD, Moran N, Horne A. Policing Major Events: Perspectives from Around the World. 1st ed. Boca Raton, FL: CRC Press; 2015

[12] Winton R. How the Rodney King beating 'banished' the baton from the LAPD. [Online]. 2016. Available at: https://www.latimes.com/local/california/la-me-rodney-king-baton-20160303-story.html. [Accessed 2019 February 2018].

[13] Kennedy WC. Police departments: Organization and tasks in disaster. American Behavioral Scientist. 1970;**13**(3):354-361. DOI: 10.1177/000276427001300305

[14] Ketchell M. The New Orleans Police Department was troubled long before Hurricane Katrina. [Online]. 2015. Available at: http://theconversation.com/the-new-orleans-police-department-was-troubled-long-before-hurricane-katrina-46381. [Accessed 2019 July 15].

[15] Sims B. The day after the Hurricane': Infrastructure, order, and the New Orleans Police Department's Response to Hurricane Katrina. Social Studies of Science. 2007;**37**(1):111-118

[16] Cha AE. New Orleans Police Keep Public Trust, Private Pain. [Online]. 2005a. Available from: https://www.washingtonpost.com/archive/

politics/2005/09/12/new-orleans-police-keep-public-trust-private-pain/f539fa07-d7a1-4efa-b7ad-a68e6d9bd9a8/. [Accessed: 6 August 2019]

[17] Anderson W. "This Isn't Representative of Our Department:" Lessons from Hurricane Katrina for Police Disaster Response Planning. [Online]. 2019. Available from: https://www.law.berkeley.edu/library/resources/disasters/Anderson.pdf. [Accessed: 31 July 2019]

[18] Baum D. Deluged: When Katrina hit, where were the police? [Online]. 2006. Available from: https://www.newyorker.com/magazine/2006/01/09/deluged. [Accessed 15 July 2019]

[19] Treaster JP Storm and crisis: Law enforcement; police quitting, overwhelmed by Chaos. The New York Times; 2022

[20] Horne J. Breach of Faith: Hurricane Katrina and the Near Death of a Great American City. NY: Random House; 2006

[21] Sims B. Disrupted Cities: Infrastructure, Social Order, and the Police Response to Hurricane Katrina. 1st ed. New York: Routledge; 2010

[22] Juvenal from his Satires (Satire VI, lines 347-348), 2022

[23] Carr D. More Horrible Than Truth: News Reports. [Online]. 2005. Available at: https://www.nytimes.com/2005/09/19/business/media/more-horrible-than-truth-news-reports.html. [Accessed 4 August 2019]

[24] Select Bipartisan Committee. A Failure of Initiative: Final Report of the Select Bipartisan Committee to Investigate the Preparation for and Response to Hurricane Katrina Report by the Select Bipartisan Committee to Investigate the Preparation for and Response to Hurricane Katrina. Washington D.C: U.S. Government Printing Office; 2006

[25] Wachtendorf T. Improvising 9/11: Organizations Improvisation following the World Trade Center. Newark, Delaware: University of Delaware; 2004